Dearest Elaine

Happy 60th! And [...] [...]ing
of a new era in you[...] [...].

With all our love
Jub, MJ, Annie
+ Becca xx.

MARGARET ROBERTS'
A-Z *of* HERBS

MARGARET ROBERTS' A-Z of HERBS

Published by Struik Nature
(an imprint of Random House Struik (Pty) Ltd)
Reg. No. 1966/003153/07
80 McKenzie Street, Cape Town, 8001 South Africa
PO Box 1144, Cape Town, 8000 South Africa

www.randomstruik.co.za

Log on to our photographic website
www.imagesofafrica.co.za
for an African experience

First edition published in 1993 by Southern Book Publishers (Pty) Ltd
Second edition published in 1997 by Southern Book Publishers (Pty) Ltd
This edition published in 2000 by Struik Publishers

ISBN 978 1 86872 499 4

10 9

Cover design by Alix Gracie, Cape Town
Illustrations by Margaret Roberts
Designed by Wim Reinders & Associates, Cape Town
Set in 10/12pt Palatino by 4-Ways DTP Services, Cape Town

Printed and bound by Times Offset (M) Sdn Bhd

PHOTOGRAPH ACKNOWLEDGEMENTS

Simpson's Nursery: pages 13, 17, 18, 19, 20, 21, 22, 27, 33,
35, 37, 39, 43, 46, 47, 48, 49, 50, 51, 52, 54, 55, 57, 60, 61, 62, 64, 65, 66, 67,
69, 70, 71, 72, 74, 76, 77, 78, 80, 81, 82, 83, 84, 86, 87, 88.

Nick Plewman: pages 14, 24, 25, 26, 28, 31, 32,
34, 42, 44, 53, 56, 58, 59, 68, 75, 79, 85.

Hortiprint: pages 15, 16, 29, 30, 38.

All photographs not acknowledged were taken by the author.

CONTENTS

INTRODUCTION

I am appalled as the years go by, to find that fewer and fewer people really read books! The computer, the video, the movie and the cassette seem to be taking over and I can only weep for future children who may miss the joy and excitement of reading a real book. Even genuine book lovers seldom have time nowadays for a leisurely read. Bearing all this in mind my publishers and I decided to produce a quick-to-read, quick-to-grasp reference book. At a glance those who have to read on the run can find what they are looking for, from A to Z. There are no frills, no anecdotes – everything is to the point! My hope is that this book will give readers a taste for herbs, encouraging them to sit down and read my more detailed books later.

May this book speed you on your busy way, but at the same time delight and inspire you to learn more about nature's little miracles, these precious herbs.

Not all herbs available in South Africa could be included in this book. New herbs are becoming available all the time, some from Europe and America, others that have been developed in South Africa. In addition, we are constantly learning more about our indigenous plants. When new plants are developed, trials and experimental recipes have to be worked through, the results logged and improvements made.

At my herbal centre at De Wildt, in the Transvaal, we have developed several new varieties of basil – a pink perennial basil, a white perennial basil, a cinnamon basil and my favourite perennial basil, which will soon be available at nurseries.

My lavenders are also developing and cross-pollinating so these, too, will be introduced soon, with new common names to identify them.

A-Z of Herbs is a quick reference book telling you the basic culinary, medicinal and cosmetic uses of the most common (and my favourite) herbs – as well as how and where to grow them. Most importantly it illustrates the herbs so that you can be sure to identify them correctly. If in doubt about the identification of a herb be sure to check with a nursery before you start using it.

ALWAYS DISCUSS ANY HOME TREATMENT WITH YOUR DOCTOR OR HOMEOPATH BEFORE YOU START USING IT.

GROWING HERBS

There is no end to the delight that growing herbs can bring you – whether you have a large, formal herb garden, a small patch of herbs outside your kitchen, a selection of herbs growing in your flower beds or just a few potted herbs on your balcony. You only really get to know herbs when you cultivate them so you should try to grow at least the common ones (once you have started you will want more and more). Store-bought dried herbs can never serve as a substitute for fresh herbs.

For each herb mentioned in this book I have given specific, concise growing instructions. If you need more detailed information or ideas for laying out your herb garden consult *Growing Herbs with Margaret Roberts*. *Indigenous Healing Plants* will guide you towards indigenous herbs to try in your garden.

I cannot emphasise enough the need to stay away from toxic insecticides when gardening with herbs – they will harm both you and the environment.

Use the following spray if your garden is infested with hungry insects, or consult *Growing Herbs with Margaret Roberts* for a comprehensive list of insect-repelling plants to grow in your garden.

Natural insect-repelling spray
southernwood
khakibos
wormwood
tansy
wilde als
seaweed (if available)
1 cup soap powder
half a cup mineral turpentine
4 cups sifted ash (made from burned newspaper, twigs and leaves)

Combine equal quantities of the herbs, chop and steep covered in boiling water. Strain. Add soap powder to 5 litres of the brew. Add turpentine and ash. Spray or splash onto the plants once a week, repeat after rain.

Insect-repelling plants
To repel aphids grow mint, nasturtium and nettle amongst your other plants. Oak leaves mulched thickly around plants will deter cutworms. Tansy will prevent fruit flies. The following can be grown amongst vegetables: marigolds, rosemary, sage, thyme, wormwood and green beans. There are also a number of indigenous plants that you can experiment with. See *Indigenous Healing Plants* for more details.

USING HERBS

Many people think that herbs are only useful in cooking – how wrong they are! For each herb I describe in this book I give as many uses as I could fit onto the page.

Domestic uses

Herbs can be used for endless purposes around the house – basil will keep flies away and a vase of rosemary sprays will deter mosquitoes. Garlic will repel weevils and a mixture of crushed cloves and lavender will protect your books and clothes from fish moths.

Many herbs can be used in potpourri to freshen your house or as a gift at Christmastime. There are hundreds of ways to make potpourri, but my favourite basic ingredients are rose petals, lavender, scented geranium leaves, lemon verbena leaves and fragrant flowers such as honeysuckle, jasmine and violets. You will need a fixative such as orange or lemon peel, powdered orris root or crushed vanilla pods. Finely ground cinnamon, cloves and nutmeg and an essential oil of your choice will complete the mixture – but the variations are endless.

Cosmetic uses

Herbs have been used in herbal preparation since time immemorial. There is a herbal remedy for all your cosmetic problems – from lanky hair to discoloured teeth. Rosemary works wonders for the hair while watercress improves the complexion. Cosmetic uses of each herb are mentioned where applicable.

Quick bath oil

This can also be used as a massage oil.
Select your herb – for example lavender, scented geranium, calendula or lemon verbena. Place one cup of leaves and flowers in the top of a double boiler, add one cup of sweet oil or almond oil. Heat gently and simmer with the lid on for 20 minutes. Give it an occasional stir with a wooden spoon. Then strain through muslin, discard the herbs and store in a clean, corked bottle.

Medicinal uses

I must reiterate that before you undertake any home remedies you must discuss them with your doctor or homeopath.

The most common way to take herbs medicinally is as a tea, and the following is the recipe for a standard brew:

Standard brew tea

Pour 1 cup of boiling water over a quarter of a cup of herbs, let it stand for five minutes, then strain. You may want to add a touch of honey or a slice of lemon.

One can also include fresh herbs in the diet to alleviate particular ailments; the chart on pages 10 and 11 lists ailments that can be treated with the herbs mentioned in this book. I have not included fruit and vegetables, but they, too, have healing properties and so deserve a place with herbs. Here is a list of some of the fruit and vegetables that should be included in the diet to cure or prevent particular ailments:

APPLES: anaemia, asthma, cataracts, diarrhoea, insomnia, stomach cramps, worms

APRICOTS: anaemia, appetite loss, asthma, bronchitis, constipation

ASPARAGUS: appetite loss, arthritis, baldness, bladder ailments, bronchitis, constipation

BEANS: appetite loss, arthritis, bronchitis, constipation, fatigue, headaches

BEETROOT: anaemia, appetite loss, arthritis, cataracts, constipation, gout, headaches, stomach cramps

BROCCOLI: anaemia, appetite loss, bronchitis, cataracts, colds, constipation, depression, high blood pressure, stomach cramps

CABBAGE: anaemia, appetite loss, arteriosclerosis, asthma, backache, baldness, bladder ailments, bronchitis, cataracts, constipation, depression, eczema, fatigue, gout, insomnia, stomach cramps

CARROTS: appetite loss, arthritis, asthma, bronchitis, cancer, cataracts, colds, ear infections, high blood pressure, insomnia, stomach cramps

CAULIFLOWER: anaemia, asthma, biliousness, colds, constipation, gout, high blood pressure
FIGS: abscesses, asthma, baldness, constipation, gout
GRAPEFRUIT: anaemia, cataracts, colds, fever
ORANGES: appetite loss, colds
POTATOES: abscesses, bronchitis, constipation, depression, diarrhoea, insomnia
PUMPKIN: abscesses, anaemia, arthritis, low blood pressure
SPINACH: anaemia, arteriosclerosis, baldness, bladder ailments, bronchitis, colds, constipation, ear infection, high blood pressure, insomnia
TOMATOES: anaemia, baldness, high cholesterol, colds, constipation, depression, gout, headaches, insomnia

Culinary uses

Unfortunately in such a concise book there was insufficient space to give recipes using all of the herbs, so the reader will have to consult my *Herbs and Spices Cookbook* for detailed recipes. An easy way to use herbs in the kitchen is in a flavoured oil or vinegar.

To make a herb oil

Use almond oil or a sweet oil for cosmetic purposes and sunflower oil for culinary purposes.

Dry the herb by hanging it upside down the shade or by placing it on newspaper in the shade and turning daily. Add it to the oil – the usual quantity is half herb, half oil– and stand in a warm place in winter. Give it a daily shake. After 10 days strain through muslin. Discard the herbs and again add freshly dried herbs (of the same variety); repeat until you get the strength you desire.

To make a herb vinegar

Fill a bottle with the herb of your choice and then fill the bottle up with white grape vinegar or a white wine vinegar. Use only fresh herbs when making a vinegar. Place the bottle in the sun for three weeks. During that time strain and replace the old herb with fresh sprigs and leaves of the same herb. Do this three or four times until you have the flavour you desire.

The chart on pages 8 and 9 will show you which herbs are best used with which foods.

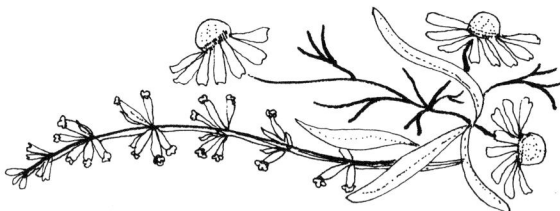

THE SELECTION OF HERBS FOR THIS BOOK

The selection of herbs for inclusion in *A-Z of Herbs* was an impossibly difficult task. I wanted to achieve a balance between being as comprehensive as possible and not overwhelming the reader with too many herbs which would defeat the object of a quick and easy to use introduction to herbs.

The herbs featured on the following three pages were not included in the main selection of herbs, but I feel it is important that readers know how to identify them correctly because I often talk about them in lectures, workshops and on television.

Burdock
Arctium lappa

This biennial herb, which produces deep maroon flowers is becoming increasingly important in the treatment of psoriasis.

Costmary
Chrysanthemum balsamita

Costmary is an old-fashioned herb which is gaining popularity in South Africa. It is an effective insect repellent and can be used to treat colds, upset stomachs, cramps and to ease childbirth.

Cotton Lavender
Santolina chamaecyparissus

A perennial herb with pretty yellow flowers which dry easily, cotton lavender is an extremely effective repellent for fish moths.

Golden Rod
Solidago virgaurea

Golden rod is an old-fashioned herb with renowned medicinal properties. It is used to treat digestive problems, kidney and bladder infections, hayfever, respiratory infections, eye ailments and makes a wonderful wound dressing.

Horseradish
Armoracia lapathifolia

Horseradish has been used in cooking and medicinally through the ages. It is an antibiotic and works particularly well on the respiratory tract and urinary system. It is effective on external and internal tumours, it stimulates the appetite and expels parasites from the digestive tract.

Hyssop
Hyssopus officinalis

A compact perennial shrub, hyssop is an asset in any garden. It is useful for soothing rheumatism and the treatment of coughs, colds and asthma.

Stinging Nettle
Urtica dioica

Despite the stinging nettle's unfriendly reputation, it has many medicinal properties. It is a diuretic, a laxative, useful for skin conditions such as eczema, it lowers the blood sugar level and is a blood cleanser and tonic.

Verbascum (Mullein)
Verbascum thapsus

Verbascum is a undemanding biennial which produces a magnificent spire of yellow flowers in its second year. It is effective in the treatment of chest ailments, earache, urinary infections and bowel complaints.

Vinca Rosea (Pink Periwinkle)
Vinca rosea

This pretty plant grows prolifically in even the harshest conditions. Research is being conducted into the use of the root in the treatment of leukaemia. Vinca rosea tea is effective for relief of rheumatism and arthritis.

CULINARY HERB CHART

	SOUPS	STOCKS, GRAVIES	SAUCES, STUFFINGS	SALADS	SALAD DRESSINGS	ROOT VEGETABLES	VEGETABLE	GARNISHING	SAVOURY RICE, PASTA	DAIRY	EGG	MEAT	FISH	POULTRY	PUDDINGS	BAKING BREADS	JAMS, JELLY SYRUPS	VINEGARS, PICKLES	TEAS, COOLDRINKS
ANGELICA			★					★		★					★	★	★		★
ANISE			★			★	★		★	★					★	★	★	★	
BALM, LEMON			★			★	★	★	★	★			★		★	★	★		★
BASIL	★	★	★	★	★	★	★	★	★	★	★	★	★	★		★		★	
BAY		★	★		★			★	★		★	★	★	★				★	
BERGAMOT			★			★				★					★	★		★	★
BORAGE	★	★		★			★	★	★		★		★	★		★		★	★
CARAWAY		★	★		★		★	★	★	★	★	★	★	★	★	★		★	★
CELERY	★	★	★	★	★			★	★		★	★	★	★				★	
CHAMOLIME										★					★	★	★		★
CHERVIL	★	★	★	★	★	★	★	★	★	★	★	★	★	★				★	★
CHIVES	★	★	★	★	★	★	★	★	★	★	★	★	★	★				★	
CORIANDER	★		★		★		★		★	★		★		★	★	★		★	
DANDELION	★		★	★			★	★	★		★	★	★	★				★	
DILL	★	★	★	★	★	★	★	★	★		★	★	★	★		★		★	★
ELDER							★		★						★	★	★		★
FENNEL	★	★	★	★	★		★	★	★	★	★	★	★	★		★		★	★
GARLIC	★	★	★	★	★	★	★		★	★	★	★	★	★	★			★	
GERANIUM, SCENTED							★		★						★	★	★		★
LAVENDER										★		★			★	★	★		★
LEMON VERBENA															★	★	★		★

	SOUPS	STOCKS, GRAVIES	SAUCES, STUFFINGS	SALADS	SALAD DRESSINGS	ROOT VEGETABLES	VEGETABLE	GARNISHING	SAVOURY RICE, PASTA	DAIRY	EGG	MEAT	FISH	POULTRY	PUDDINGS	BAKING BREADS	JAMS, JELLY SYRUPS	VINEGARS, PICKLES	TEAS, COOLDRINKS
LOVAGE	★	★	★	★	★	★	★	★	★	★	★	★	★	★				★	
MARJORAM	★	★	★	★	★	★	★	★	★	★	★	★	★	★				★	
MINT VARIETIES			★	★	★	★	★	★	★	★		★			★	★	★	★	★
MUSTARD		★	★		★				★	★	★	★	★	★				★	
NASTURTIUM	★				★	★	★		★	★		★		★	★				★
OREGANO	★	★	★		★	★		★	★	★	★	★	★	★				★	
PARSLEY	★	★	★	★	★	★	★	★	★	★	★	★	★	★				★	
ROSE			★					★		★					★	★	★		★
ROSEMARY		★	★		★	★	★	★	★	★	★	★	★	★	★	★	★	★	★
SAGE		★	★		★				★	★	★	★	★	★				★	★
SALAD BURNET	★	★			★	★		★	★		★	★		★				★	
WINTER & SUMMER SAVORY	★	★	★	★	★		★	★	★	★	★	★	★	★		★		★	
SORREL	★	★	★	★	★	★	★	★	★		★	★	★	★				★	★
TANSY										★	★		★	★	★	★	★	★	
TARRAGON	★	★	★	★	★	★	★	★	★		★	★	★	★				★	
THYME		★	★	★	★	★	★	★	★	★	★	★	★	★				★	
VIOLET				★				★		★					★	★	★		★
WATERCRESS	★	★	★	★	★	★	★	★	★	★	★	★	★	★				★	
YARROW	★	★	★		★		★	★			★	★	★	★					

THERAPEUTIC PLANTS FOR COMMON AILMENTS

Abdominal pain	mint
Abscess	bergamot
Acidosis	dandelion greens, parsley
Acne	nasturtium, elder, comfrey, salad burnet
Alcoholism	sunflower seeds
Anaemia	dandelion greens, mustard greens, parsley, watercress
Antibiotic	garlic, nasturtium, thyme
Antiseptic	mustard greens
Arteries, hardening	garlic, thyme, watercress, parsley
Arteriosclerosis	watercress, celery, parsley, lovage, borage, comfrey, salad burnet
Arthritis	celery, comfrey, garlic, mustard, parsley, sunflower seeds, mustard greens
Asthma	celery, garlic, comfrey
Backache	comfrey
Biliousness	mint, rosemary, lemon balm
Bladder ailments	celery, borage, parsley, mustard greens
Bladder stones	celery
Bleeding	parsley, yarrow, watercress, comfrey
Boils	nasturtium, onion
Bronchitis	dandelion, elderberry, garlic, bergamot, comfrey, mustard greens, onion, parsley, watercress
Cartilages	parsley, watercress
Cataracts	dandelion, watercress
Catarrh	garlic, parsley, sage, thyme
Cholesterol	borage, parsley
Circulation, poor	dandelion greens, comfrey
Colds	dandelion greens, elderberry, garlic, parsley, sage, rosemary, mustard, winter savory, watercress
Complexion	celery, borage
Conjunctivitis	dandelion greens, mustard, parsley, watercress
Constipation	celery, dandelion, onion, fennel, violet
Coughs	dandelion greens, mustard greens, parsley, watercress, lemon balm, lovage, thyme
Cramps	rosemary
Dandruff	dandelion, watercress, celery, parsley, rosemary
Depression	lemon balm, lavender
Diarrhoea	geranium (scented), yarrow
Digestion	garlic, mint, sage, peppermint
Dizziness	onion, rosemary, mint, lemon balm
Dysentery	scented geranium
Dyspepsia	mint, parsley
Ear infections	dandelion greens, mustard greens, watercress
Eczema	salad burnet, dandelion greens
Emaciation	dandelion greens
Emotional upsets	sage, rosemary, lemon balm, lavender
Energy loss	dandelion greens, mustard greens, parsley, rosemary, watercress, sunflower seeds
Eyesight	dandelion, onion, borage, calendula, chicory, tansy, watercress, nasturtium
Fainting	rosemary, sunflower seeds
Fatigue	thyme, borage, watercress
Fertility	parsley, comfrey
Fever	parsley, watercress
Flatulence	garlic, angelica, lemon verbena, tarragon, caraway, mustard

Gallstones	parsley
Genito-urinary system ailments	dandelion greens, watercress, borage, parsley, tansy, celery
Goitre	thyme
Gonorrhoea	dandelion greens, onion, garlic
Gum ailments	parsley, watercress, sage, oregano
Hair	rosemary, sage, onion, watercress, sweet-basil, bergamot
Halitosis	mint, sage, rosemary, comfrey, parsley
Headaches	rosemary, violet, borage, lavender
High blood pressure	garlic, parsley
Impotence	comfrey
Indigestion	rosemary, mint, lavender, nasturtium, oregano, lemon verbena, lemon thyme, anise, angelica, chicory, coriander, fennel, dill, caraway
Infections	chives, garlic, watercress, comfrey, mustard
Influenza	sage, comfrey, mustard, onion, winter savory, thyme, violet
Insect bites	borage, comfrey, mint
Insomnia	celery, lemon balm, lavender, onion, scented geranium
Irritability	sunflower seeds, watercress, borage, comfrey
Jaundice	elderberry, parsley, rosemary
Joint pain	parsley, watercress
Kidney stones	parsley, thyme
Kidneys	celery, dandelion greens, borage, parsley, watercress
Lactation	dandelion greens, mustard greens, parsley, watercress
Liver	onion, parsley, watercress, comfrey, borage, nasturtium, celery
Low blood pressure	dandelion greens, onion
Lumbago	comfrey
Lung ailments	comfrey, sage, thyme, celery, dandelion greens, mustard greens
Menstruations	parsley, yarrow, celery
Muscular pain	comfrey, rosemary
Nails	dandelion, onion, sunflower seeds
Nervousness	lemon balm, nasturtium, lavender, scented geranium
Obesity	celery, onion, parsley, watercress, fennel, celery, dandelion greens, mustard greens
Osteoporosis	dandelions greens, parsley, watercress
Perspiration, lack of	elderberry
Pimples	salad burnet, nasturtium, elder, comfrey
Pleurisy	onion, comfrey, violet
Restlessness	lemon balm, lavender
Rheumatism	asparagus, dandelion greens, comfrey, mustard greens, parsley, watercress, garlic, yarrow
Scalp conditions	rosemary, sweet basil, bergamot, dandelion greens
Sinusitis	mint, onion
Skin	calendula, dandelion greens, watercress, nasturtium, elder, comfrey, salad burnet
Sterility	dandelion greens, mustard greens, watercress
Stomach cramps	lemon balm, lemon verbena, dandelion greens, sage, fennel
Teeth	dandelion greens, mustard greens, parsley, watercress
Underweight	dandelion greens, comfrey, elder, thyme
Urination, painful	parsley, celery
Urinary tract diseases	parsley, borage, salad burnet, fennel, celery
Voice, hoarseness	dandelion greens, mustard greens, nasturtium, marjoram, sage, thyme, tarragon, rosemary, yarrow, bergamot
Vomiting	mint, bergamot
Worms	onion, rosemary, sweet basil, garlic, nasturtium
Wounds	bergamot, calendula, comfrey, nasturtium, thyme, sage, elder, violet, sorrel

May this book speed you on your busy way, but at the same time delight and inspire you to learn more about nature's little miracles, these precious herbs.

AFRICAN MARIGOLD/ (STINK) AFRIKANER
Tagetes erecta
Family: Compositae

The marigold plants are characterised by their bright orange and yellow flowers and their ability to deter certain garden insects and worms. They are a gay and useful addition to any garden and grow without fuss in most South African gardens. They are indigenous to Mexico, despite their name, and the Aztecs used them extensively for medicinal and culinary purposes many centuries ago. They have now come back into favour, largely because of their amazing insect repelling properties.

CULTIVATION
The African marigold is an annual plant.

Conditions: The plant likes sunny positions, and an average well-drained soil. It's one of the most unfussy plants in cultivation!

Propagation: From seed. Sow seeds in trays or seedbeds in August and keep well watered. Prepare a bed that is dug deeply and well composted, with 3 to 4 spadefuls per square metre. Water well and plant out seedlings when they are big enough to handle. Shade them by pressing a few leafy twigs around the seedlings for a few days. Keep moist until they become sturdy, then water once a week or more often if they wilt in the summer heat. Plant the smaller variety 20 to 30 cm apart and the larger variety 60 cm apart.

Containers: The African marigold can be grown in containers in full sun.

Size: 15 to 90 cm, depending on type.

Harvesting: Use flowers and leaves all through the summer for insect control. The more you pick the more they bloom.

Dos and don'ts: Marigolds make the perfect edging plants for vegetable gardens as they deter insect pests. They will, however, attract bees to the garden. Do grow them between rows of tomatoes; they seem to increase the fruit yield and will keep away flies. Grow all over the garden to keep it insect-free all summer long. I alternate a row of lettuce, a row of marigolds, a row of tomatoes, a row of basil, a row of radishes and a row of miniature marigolds for an insect-free feast – and a visual one, too.

USES
Domestic
☐ Marigolds dug into the soil before planting potatoes will deter nematodes. They are definitely worth planting as a soil-building crop.

☐ Feed a few marigold leaves and flowers to chickens to give their flesh and egg yolk a good colour, but do so in moderation otherwise you may upset their digestion.

☐ Add dried marigold flowers and leaves to potpourris and insect repellent sachets. Khakibos, a close relative of the marigold, is also invaluable as an insect repellent and becomes pleasantly aromatic when dried. Dried khakibos plants should be saved for the compost heap as they rid it of unwanted egg-laying insects. Khakibos or khakiweed (*Tagetes minuata*) originated in South America and was transported to South Africa in horse bedding and feed. The oil is extracted for the perfume industry and exported all over the world. As it is one of the most useful of all insect repelling plants, it is a welcome weed everywhere.

Cosmetic
☐ Crushed marigold petals are used by several African tribes to clear up pimples.

ALOE/AALWYN
Aloe vera, Aloe ferox
Family: Liliaceae

Aloe vera

There are over 350 species of aloes.

Aloes are a familiar sight in South Africa where they grow in many inhospitable and bleak places, lending a splash of colour to the landscape. The juice of Aloe ferox, among many other species, has long been used by the indigenous peoples for medicinal purposes, and the Dutch colonists were quick to adopt its use, employing it mainly as a wound dressing. Now Aloe ferox is gaining increasing acceptance in modern medicine.

The sap of Aloe vera has become widely used as an ingredient in cosmetics and beauty preparations, particularly shampoos, creams and suntan preparations. Cleopatra herself is said to have used it in her beauty preparations. It has the ability to heal radiation burns. The sap must be fresh, however, as it loses its properties with age.

CULTIVATION
Aloes are generally very hardy and grow especially well in dry, warm areas. *A. ferox* is particularly spectacular as a garden plant and looks very good in rockeries.
Conditions: Aloes like a sunny location, with poor, well-drained soil, and grow best in frost-free areas.
Propagation: By seeds. The seeds should be planted in spring in sand-filled trays. They germinate quickly and easily and need only be kept moist until big enough to handle. They need sun from an early age so make sure

the seedlings get enough warmth and light until they are established, then plant out 30 cm apart in well-dug soil to which a little old manure has been added. Thereafter they need only an occasional watering. In areas of heavy frost the flower may suffer damage but on the whole aloes are tough and undemanding.
Containers: *Aloe vera* makes an excellent indoor plant as long as it has a sunny window sill.
Size: Aloes grow to 3 m.
Harvesting: Leaves can be cut off as required, preferably from plants at least two years old.

USES
Domestic
The juice of *Aloe ferox* is used to get rid of ticks in cattle and dogs, and to treat scab on sheep.

Cosmetic
☐ The sap of *Aloe vera* can be used to make an excellent moisturising cream.
☐ Mix *Aloe vera* sap into shampoos to soothe dry or itchy scalps. Add to suntan creams for its soothing properties.

Medicinal
☐ The juice of *Aloe ferox* is useful as a purgative. Use 2-3 pinches of dried juice in 150 ml warm milk and sweeten with honey or molasses.

The Zulu and Xhosa people sometimes mix aloe juice with mealie meal or clay and eat it as a purge.
☐ Aloe juice is also effective for expelling worms and relieving constipation and indigestion. It should not, however, be used by anyone suffering from piles as it draws blood to the large intestine.
☐ Aloe juice can also be applied to burns, scalds, rashes and heat rash. First shave off the spiked borders of the leaf and cut the leaf crossways, then apply the fresh, sticky juice directly to the affected area. It is very bitter, but can also be used for mouth ulcers.
☐ *Aloe vera* leaves can be crushed and used as a poultice for chapped skin, skin disorders and burns.

Culinary
☐ Some aloe leaves can be made into a delicious jam.

Aloe vera

ANGELICA/ENGELKRUID OF ENGELWORTEL

Angelica archangelica
Family: Umbelliferae

Angelica is familiar to most people as a green crystallised cake decoration, made from the stems of the plant. It features prominently in old legends and particularly in the folklore of Lapland, Iceland and Russia. Angelica was used in pagan rites and later in Christian festivals. It gives a sensation of warmth when eaten – which is perhaps why it is so highly prized in cold countries.

The plant may have been named "angelic" in medieval times because of its healing properties, or it may have been so called because it usually came into bloom around the feast day of the Archangel Michael.

Angelica also has medicinal properties, it is now used in homeopathy and to make medicinal teas.

CULTIVATION

Angelica is a very attractive biennial that makes a good focal point in the garden.

Conditions: It prefers semi-shade and a light alkaline soil, and thrives in moist conditions.

Propagation: From fresh seed only. The seeds should be sown in spring. Plant the seedlings out in well-composted soil, 120 cm apart. Water them well and keep shaded until established. The plant flowers in its second year and if the flowers are clipped off it will go on flowering for several years. Once the plant has flowered it begins to die, so it can be pulled up at this stage. If the seeds look mature they can be planted at once in time for the next season.

Size: The angelica plant grows to a height of between 1 and 1,5 m, including the flowering head.

Harvesting: Cut the stems before midsummer for crystallising. Harvest the leaves before flowering, and collect ripe seed in late summer.

Dos and don'ts: Because of its height angelica is best placed at the back of the garden. Do check the plants for aphids, as angelica is prone to infestation. Angelica will attract bees to your garden.

USES

Domestic

☐ The leaves and stems can be chopped up and dried, and used in potpourris as a fixative. Make an incision at the crown of the plant to yield an aromatic gum, which can also be used as a potpourri fixative when dried.

☐ The dried seed heads look very striking in flower arrangements. The long-stemmed leaves are also suitable for vase arrangements.

☐ Angelica seeds can be burned to perfume a room.

Cosmetic

☐ Put angelica leaves in the bath for a relaxing soak.

Medicinal

☐ Combat flatulence by slowly chewing a piece of angelica stalk.

☐ Angelica offers protection against infection, soothes digestion and improves circulation and respiration.

☐ The aroma of the crushed leaves in a car helps prevent travel sickness.

Culinary

☐ Angelica is best known in the form of crystallised stems, used for cake decoration.

☐ The young leaves can be chopped to give a mild, fresh taste to salads. Fresh stalks can be added to milk puddings, custards and stewed fruits. They also remove the tartness from rhubarb and apples if placed in the pan while these fruits are cooking.

☐ Finely chopped angelica leaves and stems can be used in fruit salads.

☐ The midribs of the large leaves can be eaten like celery and the seeds can be used in spice mixtures.

☐ Angelica adds a subtle flavour to dry white wine if you steep a stalk and a leaf or two before serving. It has long been used to flavour wines, vermouth and some liqueurs such as Chartreuse.

☐ Angelica combines well with mint, ginger, cinnamon and vanilla.

☐ Angelica can be used to make a delicious ice-cream.

ANISE/ANYS

Pimpinella anisum
Family: Umbelliferae

Anise or aniseed has probably been cultivated for thousands of years. It was indigenous to the regions east of the Mediterranean, and the ancient Egyptians grew it in abundance for culinary and medicinal use. The Romans were especially fond of it, and used it as a main ingredient in a special cake, Mustaceus, which also contained cumin and other digestive herbs. It is thought that it was the precursor of wedding cakes. Anise is particularly valuable as a digestive herb, which is why it is so often used in cooking – particularly for the elderly and people with delicate stomachs. The anise fruit is the part known as aniseed. It is very small and brown, with a distinctive licorice flavour. It is used to flavour anisette liqueur.

CULTIVATION

Anise is an annual herbaceous plant.

Conditions: Likes sunny and sheltered locations, and a light well-drained and alkaline soil.

Propagation: By sowing seeds, preferably in situ, long after the danger of frost has passed. It does not transplant very easily because it has a taproot. If they are to be transplanted, sow seeds in cardboard egg boxes. Fill with sand, sow each seed individually and keep damp until the seedlings appear. When they are big enough tear away the excess cardboard around the egg box and plant them, board and all, into the garden. This ensures that the seeds are not disturbed; the cardboard will soon disintegrate. Transplant to about 60 cm apart. The flat white flower heads bloom in midsummer. The seedlings must be well protected – water regularly.

Size: Grows up to 30 cm in height

Harvesting: Lower leaves can be picked as required; flowers as they open. When the plant starts turning grey-green at the tips it should be cut at ground level. Suspend plants until the seeds are ripe and gather seeds. Gather stems and dig up roots in autumn. I often leave the seeds to ripen on the plant to provide fresh seed for next season.

Dos and don'ts: Do plant anise between rows of spinach, lettuce and tomatoes.

USES

Domestic

☐ The seed can be used as bait in mousetraps.

☐ The seed can be added to potpourris – it acts as an excellent fixative for the essential oils.

☐ Anise is an ingredient in a natural fish moth repellent. Add 1 cup each of crushed aniseed, cloves, roughly crushed whole nutmeg, cinnamon pieces and coriander seeds to 2 cups of lavender flowers. Add lavender and clove essential oils, then shake up in a large sealed jar. Store for a week then fill sachets, envelopes, etc. with the mixture and place in cupboards. Add more oil from time to time.

Cosmetic

☐ Grind the seed and add to face packs.

☐ The oil from the seed is used in perfumes, toothpaste, soap and mouthwashes.

☐ Chew the slightly roasted seed to sweeten breath.

Medicinal

☐ The seed may be infused to make an antiseptic tea to soothe sore throats, coughs, colds and bronchial problems. It also relieves colic in babies and if taken by nursing mothers increases their milk. Pour a cup of boiling water over 2 tsp lightly crushed seed, stand for 5 minutes then stir and strain. Give 1 tsp at a time to colicky babies.

Culinary

☐ The seed can be used in breads, cakes, pies, cream and confectionery. Use it whole or in crushed form.

☐ Anise complements savoury dishes including pickles, curries and cream cheeses.

☐ The flower can be added to fruit salads.

☐ The leaf can be added in small quantities to fruit salads and green salads.

☐ The stem and root may be mixed into soups and stews; it has a slight licorice flavour.

BAY/LOURIERSTRUIK
Laurus nobilis
Family: Lauraceae

The bayleaf is widely used for culinary purposes and is so versatile that a bay tree should be a feature in every herb garden. The bayleaf has also been used medicinally for thousands of years, but its symbolic associations were even more significant than its practical uses. The bay tree was sacred to the Greek god Apollo. His temple at Adelphi had a roof made of bayleaves for it was believed they had a protective effect against evil influences and lightning.

The Romans thought very highly of the bay, and in fact it became a symbol of excellence. Athletes and poets were crowned with bay wreaths, and since then a laurel wreath has been regarded as a sign of honour. It is still used today to crown victorious sportsmen and outstanding symphony conductors. The plant's Latin name comes from the words "laurus," meaning "laurel," and "nobilis," meaning "renowned."

CULTIVATION
The bay tree is a perennial evergreen.
Conditions: The bay likes full sun, and should be sheltered from the wind. It grows well in an average, moist soil that is well drained.
Propagation: Take cuttings from the previous season's growth by pulling off a small "heel" at the base of the stem. Dip into a rooting hormone. Plant the cuttings in boxes and keep them well watered in a cool place. You can make a "tent" for the boxes out of clear plastic, supported on wires so it is well clear of the plants. Allow the cuttings to harden off in the sun for a week or two before transplanting directly into the garden. Leave plenty of space between them as in frost-free areas bay trees grow very large.
Containers: It makes an ideal container plant, but the pot should be large as it does not like to be disturbed, and it must be in full sun.
Size: Reaches a height of 7 m.
Harvesting: The leaves can be picked any time and used fresh or dried.
Dos and don'ts: If you live in a cold area the tree will need some winter protection.

USES
Domestic
☐ The leaves have been made into wreaths for thousands of years.
☐ A dried bayleaf sprig placed in flour and dried foods will keep weevils away.
☐ The leaves can be hung up in a room to keep the air fresh.

Cosmetic
☐ Add a decoction of the leaf to bathwater for a revitalising effect. It makes a superb footbath. Boil 2 cups of fresh leaves in 2 *l* of water for 15 minutes, then cool until pleasantly warm. Strain, and soak the feet in it for 15 minutes.

Medicinal
☐ An infusion of the leaf serves as an appetite stimulant and aid to digestion. Pour a cup of boiling water over one bayleaf, let it stand for 5 minutes and strain.
☐ The essential oil of bayleaf soothes sprains and rheumatic joints.
☐ The crushed berries, mixed with aqueous cream, make a soothing rub for sprains and bruises. They should not be eaten as they are poisonous.

Culinary
☐ The leaf is used in bouquet garni and to flavour savoury dishes such as casseroles, soups, marinades, sauces, stuffing, curries, etc. It imparts its flavour slowly over a long period, which is why it is so good in dishes that take a long time to cook. Always remove the leaf before serving, as it can become bitter.
☐ Add the leaf to custards and rice puddings for a subtle flavour. A few fresh leaves stored in rice will give it a pleasant taste.

BASIL/BASIELKRUID
Ocimum basilicum
Family: Labiatae

Sweet basil

Basil is one of the most versatile herbs and one of the standards that no herb grower can really afford to do without. Sweet basil is the most popular variety, but dark opal basil is increasing in popularity as it is more decorative and can still be used in cooking. Basil has been cultivated for more than 4 000 years. A perennial variety grows in India, "Ocimum sanctum," holy basil or sacred basil. In South Africa it is generally treated as a tender annual as it is susceptible to frost. In India it is regarded as a sacred herb and is used for decorating temples. It was widely used in ancient Rome and Greece. Its name derives from the Basilisk, a mythical serpent-like creature whose venom was so potent it could kill just by looking. The herb was said to be an antidote to the poison. It is believed to have been found growing around Christ's tomb after the resurrection, and for this reason some Greek Orthodox churches use it to prepare holy water and grow it below the church altar. Basil has a pungent, spicy scent and enhances many savoury dishes.

CULTIVATION
Basil is a tender annual that is susceptible to frost.
Conditions: Basil likes sun, but prefers semi-shade in midsummer, and an average soil.
Propagation: From seeds. Sow seed in trays in August and keep protected until all danger of frost is past. Once seedlings reach the four-leaf stage they can easily be transplanted. Place 50 cm apart and keep shaded for a day or two. Put a little compost on to keep the roots cool. Water regularly to promote growth.
Containers: Basil can be grown on sunny window sills in large pots in winter. It needs 7 hours of sun a day. Bear in mind that basil is an annual, however, and the perennial varieties are more suitable for this purpose.
Size: Grows to between 30 and 60 cm.
Harvesting: The leaves can be removed any time, but preferably when young. Take off the tops as the flowers open. The whole plant can be dried at the start of winter. The leaves may be removed as required for culinary use and the seed heads taken off for potpourris.
Dos and don'ts: Do plant basil if you want to attract butterflies to your garden. Do not plant it near rue, as they dislike each other. Plant between rows of tomatoes, between squashes, pumpkins, cucumbers and green peppers. It enhances all their flavours and keeps insects away.

USES
Domestic
☐ Dried basil seed heads make attractive additions to dry flower arrangements, and will give the room a spicy scent.
☐ Basil seed heads can be added to potpourris as fixatives.
☐ Bunches of fresh basil hung in the kitchen will keep flies away – bruise the leaves frequently.
☐ Dried basil stalks burnt on a fire deter mosquitoes.
☐ Basil leaves can be stored for winter use by drying, laying leaves in a crock with alternate layers of basil and pure coarse salt, or stored half dried in olive oil.
☐ Fresh green basil leaves kept in a bowl indoors will repel flies. Or keep a pot of basil on the kitchen window sill in the sun and bruise a few leaves every day.

Cosmetic
☐ Crushed, pounded basil leaves are said to stimulate hair growth if massaged thoroughly into the scalp. It is used for this purpose by many African tribes. Some tribes also believe that basil branches placed under a mattress will keep evil spirits away and promote sleep.
☐ Add the flowering top and leaf to baths for a fresh, invigorating infusion.

Medicinal
☐ In ancient times basil was used to draw out the poison from insect bites and stings – the crushed or pounded leaf was applied to the area.
☐ Basil is a tonic and antiseptic and excellent for the relief of nausea and as a digestive aid.
☐ Rub fresh basil leaves onto the temples to cure headaches.

☐ Basil can be used as a gargle for clearing mouth infections. Infuse six leaves in 250 ml boiling water for this purpose. Stand for 5 minutes and strain before use.

☐ Crushed basil leaves, massaged around the heels, will soothe aches and pains caused by standing for a long time. Alternatively, pour 2 l of boiling water over 2 cups of fresh leaves and leave to cool. Strain and use as a foot-bath.

Culinary

☐ Basil does not combine happily with most other herbs as its flavour is too strong, but it can safely be used with celery, parsley and mint.

☐ Basil tastes particularly good with tomatoes and makes tomato bredie a really special dish. Add a little just before serving.

☐ Basil is a good addition to salad dressing.

☐ Fresh basil pounded in a pestle with salt, garlic and olive oil, then added to pasta or other sauces is the basis for the popular Italian pesto sauce. Walnuts or pine nuts are also included in the traditional recipe.

☐ Basil can be preserved by packing it in bottles and filling them with olive oil. This oil then makes a delicious salad dressing. Basil can also be laid in a jar and covered with coarse sea salt.

☐ Add finely chopped basil to cooked vegetables like courgettes, brinjals, marrows and squash just before serving.

A perennial basil hybrid

Pesto Sauce

This classic Genoese sauce can be used on all types of pasta and it can be added to soups and stews too for an unusual taste. It is best to use fresh basil, but if it is winter and there is no basil available, use the salt-stored leaves from your crock.

large bunch fresh basil – to give 4 cups leaves
2 – 3 cloves garlic
little salt
4 tablespoons walnuts or pine nuts
4 tablespoons grated Parmesan cheese
5 – 6 tablespoons olive oil

Strip the leaves from the fresh basil and using a large pestle and mortar pound the leaves with the garlic. Add a little salt and the walnuts or pine nuts, pounding well all the time. Add the grated Parmesan cheese and pound to a smooth paste, gradually incorporating the olive oil.
Try with baked potatoes and hard-boiled eggs.

Other Varieties of Basil

Camphor basil (*Ocimum kilimandscharicum*) – a perennial named for Mount Kilimanjaro. This is a fascinating garden subject which can be clipped into a low hedge or topiary. It is used to treat fever, as an external wash for infection and as an insect repellent.

Transvaal basil (*Ocimum canum*) – a compact annual plant. An excellent treatment for coughs, colds and fevers.

Zulu basil (*Ocimum urticifolium*) – a basil with lemon-scented leaves that soothe aching feet and keep away mosquitoes.

Several varieties have recently cross-pollinated in my garden and we are making several new hybrids available at nurseries.

BERGAMOT (BEE BALM) /BERGAMOT

Monarda didyma
Family: Labiatae

This herb is indigenous to North America but became popular in Europe after early settlers brought back the seeds. It was probably named bergamot because the scent of its leaves is reminiscent of the Italian bergamot orange, from which oil of bergamot is produced. It is also known as Oswego. The North American Indians made an infusion of the herb, and it became a popular substitute for tea in New England after the Boston Tea Party in 1773. The Indians also used it to treat colds and chest complaints. It contains the antiseptic thymol. It is an excellent garden plant because it has a lovely flower and is very showy. The colours range through red, cerise, pink, magenta and, rarely, white.

CULTIVATION

Bergamot is a hardy herbaceous perennial.

Conditions: Like other members of the mint family, bergamot likes partial (afternoon) shade in hot climates. The soil should be rich, moist and light.

Propagation: By stem or root cuttings and from seed. Divide the clump every three or four years and space 60 cm apart. Cuttings should be taken from the outer edges of the clump and set in sand to root quickly. Cut back the flowering heads level with the lower leaves of the rootstock when they have finished flowering.

Winter growth is slow and will benefit from a dressing of compost.

Size: From 30 to 90 cm. In moist conditions the flowering head reaches 1 m.

Harvesting: Pick the leaves in spring or summer. Pick flowers when they open. When you cut back the plant save the leaves and flowers for potpourris.

Dos and don'ts: Do plant bergamot if you want to attract bumble bees, butterflies and bees to your garden. Honey bees are unable to reach the nectar, however, unless holes have already been made by other insects. Do plant bergamot with rosemary; together they make an attractive hedge. Plant the bergamot in front of the rosemary for best effect as the flowers will be cut down in winter. Don't let the plants dry out or they will become weak and spindly.

USES

Domestic
☐ Both the flowers and leaves make wonderful additions to potpourris.

Cosmetic
☐ The North American Indians boiled the flowering top of wild bergamot to make a hair oil. Bergamot leaves added to bath vinegars make excellent refreshers, and can be infused in hot water as a rinse for oily hair.

Medicinal
☐ The leaf can be made into an tea for nausea, flatulence, menstrual pain and insomnia. The standard brew is a cup of boiling water poured over a quarter cup of fresh leaves. Leave to stand for 5 minutes, then strain and sweeten with honey if liked.

☐ Bergamot leaf can be inhaled in steam to relieve bronchial catarrh and sore throats.

Culinary
☐ The soft petals of the flower (pulled out of the calyx) can be added to salads.

☐ If the fresh leaf is added to China tea it gives it a flavour reminiscent of Earl Grey tea, and cooled standard brew tea can be added to wine and fruit juices.

☐ The leaf can be added to stuffings or added to apple sauce as a condiment for pork.

☐ An infusion of the leaf can also be used in jams and jellies, or simmered with fruit in jam making. Remove before bottling.

☐ Sprinkle dried bergamot on veal for a delicious flavour.

☐ Bergamot can be added to cabbage dishes, rice and samp.

☐ Bergamot chopped with mint makes a tasty addition to spanspek or melon dishes. Remember, however, that it is strongly flavoured and should be used sparingly!

BULBINELLA/KATSTERT
Bulbine frutescens
Family: Liliaceae

The name Bulbinella is applied incorrectly to many members of this large group of plants, which has lead to confusion about which is the "real" one. There are several varieties of B. frutescens, some with long, thin dark green leaves, and others with pale leaves. The most common one is the yellow-flowered, juicy leaved bulbinella that is found in many South African gardens as a rockery plant. The leaves yield a jelly-like juice that has a number of instant medical applications!

CULTIVATION
Bulbinella grows quickly, easily and abundantly.
Conditions: It thrives in any soil and can be planted in awkward spots such as rocky hillsides where little else will grow. It likes full sun and needs little water but it will reward a weekly watering with profuse flowers. Dig in the odd spadeful of compost.
Propagation: Simply pull off a piece of an established plant and replant – it will soon be flowering away.
Containers: Flat dwellers can grow it in a pot on a sunny window sill or in a large tub on a balcony.
Size: Bulbinella grows to a height of about 15 cm.
Harvesting: Pick fresh leaves as required.

USES
Domestic
☐ Very useful to landscapers – it has a neat, compact growth and a mass of flowers all year round. Being succulent it withstands drought. It also survives frost, strong winds and city pollution.

Cosmetic
☐ Extracts of bulbinella juice make an excellent basis for skin creams.
☐ I often refer to bulbinella as an indigenous *Aloe vera* – it can be used in a similar way.

Medicinal
Bulbinella can be described as a natural medicine chest because it is so versatile.
☐ Bulbinella is very effective in the treatment of eczema – just squeeze the juice onto the affected area for instant relief.
☐ Apply the freshly squeezed juice of the leaves to burns, blisters, rashes, insect bites, itchy patches, cracked lips, fever blisters, cold sores, pimples, mouth ulcers, cracked skin, bee and wasp stings, and sores and rashes on animals.

BORAGE/ KOMKOMMERKRUID

Borago officinalis
Family: Boraginaceae

The borage family includes a range of very interesting plants, and it is related to comfrey, anchusa and forget-me-not. Most members of the family have mauve or blue flowers and no fragrance other than a fresh cucumber-like scent and taste. Borage has beautiful small, five-petalled flowers of a clear blue and hairy leaves. It has many culinary and medicinal uses, but has been particularly associated with the ability to make people happy and banish melancholy. It is believed to have originated in Syria but today it is cultivated all over the world and is often found growing wild. The name is derived from the Celtic word for courage. As far back as medieval times it was said that wine with borage flowers in it would give strength and joyfulness and cure fever. Borage was supposed to have been given to the Crusaders to bolster their courage. Its medicinal qualities may relate to its high content of calcium, potassium and mineral salts, and the fact that it works on the adrenal cortex of the kidney, helping it to produce its own cortisone.

CULTIVATION

Because of its multitude of uses, borage is an essential component of any herb garden. It is a hardy annual plant.

Conditions: Borage thrives in a dry, poor soil, and should be grown in full sun, but can take a little light shade.

Propagation: Borage seeds itself readily and seems to grow well in either clay or sandy soil. Plant the seeds 30-36 cm apart in tilled soil, about 1 cm below the surface, and cover with sand and a light dressing of compost to help keep the soil damp. Sow in early spring and again in midsummer.

Containers: Borage does well as a pot plant but is difficult to transplant once it reaches the four-leaf stage as it has a long taproot. It is important to use borage fresh, so new self-sown seedlings can be potted up for the sunny kitchen window sill at the end of summer to give a continuous supply of leaves during the winter.

Size: Grows to a height of 30-90 cm.

Harvesting: Pick flowers and leaves as required – it can also withstand frost and winter rains.

Dos and don'ts: If you want to encourage bees you should cultivate borage as they love the flowers. Do plant borage next to strawberries, as they thrive together. Borage helps to control the tomato worm if it is planted near tomatoes.

USES

Domestic

☐ The fresh flowers are an extremely decorative addition to summer arrangements, and to edible flower salads.

☐ Borage flowers can be preserved by crystallising, and they make an attractive decoration on cakes and puddings. Dip each flower into the white of an egg which has been beaten with a fork until opaque but not foamy. Then dip into castor sugar. Turn until the flower is completely coated. (You can leave a piece of stem on the flower for easy handling, and then snip it off after the flower has dried.) Lay the flowers on a sheet of greaseproof paper on a wire rack and leave to dry in a warm place. You can also place them in the oven at a very low heat, leaving the door slightly open. Once the flowers are dry and brittle, store them in an airtight container between layers of greaseproof paper.

Cosmetic

☐ The borage leaf can be added, finely minced, to a face pack for dry skin. It may also be mixed, again finely minced, with cooked barley and bran in a bath bag to cleanse and soften the skin.

Medicinal

☐ Borage leaf tea can be drunk to bring down a fever, and applied to tired, sore eyes. It is also said to relieve chest colds, bronchitis and coughs. Make the brew by pouring a cup of boiling water over a quarter cup of fresh leaves. Stand for five minutes then strain. Sweeten with honey if liked and sip while pleasantly warm. The brew can also be used as a gargle for sore throats.

☐ Crushed borage leaves can be rubbed into insect bites

and stings, and crushed leaves applied to swellings and bruises will have a healing effect.

☐ Borage contains potassium, which helps the body make cortisone by stimulating the adrenal cortex. It is also useful in kidney and bladder infections. It is also said to relieve stress and depression.

☐ The borage leaf is useful in salt-free diets as it is rich in mineral salts.

Culinary

☐ Borage should be used fresh as it loses its flavour when dried. It can be satisfactorily frozen, however.

☐ Borage leaf makes a delicious addition to fruit cups and fruit salads. The decorative flowers can also be added to fruit salads.

☐ The young leaves can be dipped in batter and fried to make a delicious fritter. They can also be added to soups and stews.

☐ Borage tea is a delicious and relaxing bedtime drink. Make it as indicated above, and sweeten with honey.

☐ Borage leaves can be cooked on their own in the same way as spinach, or added to spinach. They can also be finely chopped and added to soft cheeses, pickles and sandwiches.

☐ Recent medical research has indicated that borage may damage the liver. Only take borage internally with guidance from your doctor.

Borage fruit cup

10 granadillas
1 litre granadilla juice
1 cup borage flowers
little sugar or honey to sweeten
1 litre ginger ale
1 litre ginger beer

Blend and serve in a punch bowl with the borage flowers floating on top. This also freezes well and can be used to make ice lollies for children. To do this, insert a sucker stick into the ice cube sections just before it freezes solid.

SERVES 10 – 12

Borage fritters

This dish is a great favourite with everyone served with stews, curry or just a green salad and cheese.

several young borage leaves (approx. 12)
sunflower oil

Batter

1 cup flour (I use sifted brown flour)
$^1/_2$ – $^3/_4$ cup milk
1 beaten egg
sea salt and pepper
$^1/_2$ teaspoon grated nutmeg

Combine and beat the ingredients well, adding a little more milk if necessary to make a fairly liquid batter. Dip each leaf into the batter and fry in deep, hot oil until golden brown. Drain, and serve immediately while they are still hot and crisp.

SERVES 6

CALENDULA OR POT MARIGOLD/(TUIN) GOUSBLOM
Calendula officinalis
Family: Compositae

The calendula or pot marigold is both a versatile herb and gay flowering plant, widely used for cosmetic and culinary purposes, as well as for healing. Gardeners love it because it blooms freely in winter and early summer. It was used as far back as ancient Egyptian times, among other things for flavouring food and colouring commodities like butter and cheese. It is indigenous to the Mediterranean, but is now seen in gardens the world over.

CULTIVATION

The calendula is a hardy annual that deserves a prominent position in the garden because of its cheerful appearance and lengthy flowering period.

Conditions: It likes a sunny position and prefers a fine loam but will grow in most soil types unless they are waterlogged.

Propagation: Seeds can be sown in beds or pots in February and March for planting out in May/June.

Containers: The calendula makes an excellent container plant in a sunny spot outside.

Size: Grows to 20-30 cm.

Harvesting: Pick the leaves when young and flowers when they are open.

Dos and don'ts: Calendulas are best in groups and need full sun to keep them healthy. They make excellent companion plants for cabbages, winter broad beans and peas.

USES

Domestic

☐ The petals can be dried and added to potpourri for a splash of colour. Dried flowers can be used in perennial arrangements.

☐ The flowers can be boiled in water to produce a pale yellow dye.

Cosmetic

☐ Add the fresh flower petals to creams and preparations for cleansing and softening skin. They can also be added to bath water or made into hair rinses for lacklustre hair.

Medicinal

☐ The flower has soothing and antiseptic properties. It can be used in ointments for leg ulcers, varicose veins and bruises. Aqueous cream is an excellent base.

☐ Taken internally in an infusion the flower promotes digestion.

☐ An infusion of the flowers makes a healing mouthwash for gums.

☐ Calendula oil, extracted from the petals, is used in many skin preparations and aromatherapy. It soothes inflammation, chilblains, etc., and relieves sore nipples caused by breastfeeding.

☐ Calendula is a good antiseptic and skin healer. In the American Civil War doctors used the crushed leaves to treat open wounds.

☐ Include the flower in your diet if you have circulatory problems or skin disorders. The flower tea is made by pouring a cup of boiling water over 1 tablespoon of fresh petals, leaving to stand for 5 minutes and then straining. This brew can also be used as a lotion.

Culinary

☐ The flowers can be added to rice (a far cheaper alternative to saffron), soups, cheeses, yoghurt, omelettes, etc. to give a yellow colour. They can also be used to garnish fruit salad. They do not have a strong flavour so can be combined with more flavoursome herbs.

☐ Sprinkle the leaves in salads and stews, bake in scones and cakes, custards and creams, and sweet and savoury biscuits.

CARAWAY/KARWAY
Carum carvi
Family: Umbelliferae

Caraway is a biennial herb that belongs to the carrot family, as can be seen from its fernlike leaves and distinctive lacy flower heads. It is indigenous to Europe but now found wild in North Africa, parts of Asia and India. It has several medicinal uses and has been utilised for at least 5 000 years, which is known because seeds of caraway have been found in prehistoric dwelling sites. The ancient Roman and Greeks used it for digestive and tonic purposes, as well as flavouring food. Caraway was used in Elizabethan times to round off a feast, and was mentioned in this context in Shakespeare's Henry IV. The universal popularity of the herb stems from the fact that it is a sure cure for flatulence and lack of appetite, as well as a useful remedy for diarrhoea. The whole plant has its uses although the seeds are the best part for flavouring purposes. They have a distinctive licorice flavour. Besides its more prosaic uses, caraway is believed to give protection from witches and was used in love potions as it was believed to be able to prevent departures!

CULTIVATION
Conditions:
Caraway will make do in any type of soil as long as the drainage is good, but it prefers a sandy, light soil. It likes full sun.

Propagation: Caraway grows easily from seeds sown in spring, but they should be sown straight into the ground. Sow the seeds about 20 cm apart. Cover with sand and then with a light layer of compost and shade close to the ground with hessian. Keep moist until the seedlings are 5-7 cm high, then harden off by lifting the hessian for 2 hours longer each day.

Size: Up to 60 cm.

Harvesting: Seeds can be harvested when ripe and starting to dry. Leaves can be gathered when young. Pick seed heads in late summer or when the seeds turn brown, and dig up roots in the second autumn.

Dos and don'ts: Caraway is a good companion to green peas. It makes a quick low hedge around chicken runs and keeps them fly-free in summer.

USES
Domestic
☐ When added to certain odiferous foods, such as cabbage and cauliflower, caraway seeds remove the cooking smell.

☐ The caraway plant dries beautifully and is ideal for pressing and dried flower arrangements.

☐ Baked caraway dough placed in pigeon lofts is said to ensure that the pigeons will always return!

Cosmetic
☐ The essential oil from the seed is used in mouthwashes and colognes.

Medicinal
☐ The seeds can be chewed or infused to assist in digestion, relieve flatulence and sweeten breath.

Culinary
☐ A caraway tea can be made by crushing one teaspoonful of seeds per cup of boiling water, and then pouring the water over the seeds. Add a sprig of mint, steep then strain and drink sweetened with honey if desired. You can also tie two teaspoons of the seeds in a muslin bag, then place a bag in a teapot, one per person, and make it with a sprig of mint as you would after-dinner tea.

☐ The essential oil of caraway is used in confectionery and some liqueurs, including Kummel.

☐ Caraway seeds can be used to flavour meat dishes, soups, bread, cakes, biscuits, cheese, etc.

☐ The young caraway leaves and flowers can be used in salads.

☐ Caraway roots can be boiled as a vegetable and served with butter and lemon juice, and are delicious served cold with ham and asparagus.

☐ The seeds are often served with cheese after a meal because of their beneficial effect on digestion. They can also be mixed with butter or cottage cheese.

☐ Powdered caraway enhances pork dishes, meat loaf, beef stews and grilled liver and onions. A little can also be used to give a distinctive taste to home-baked bread.

CASTOR OIL PLANT/ KASTEROLIEPLANT
Ricinus communis
Family: Euphorbiaceae

The castor oil plant is not indigenous to South Africa but in some places it grows almost like a weed. Its association with the dreaded castor oil purge of childhood makes many people wary of this decorative plant! However, it needs little attention and is such a useful plant that it should have a place in every herb garden. The leaves of the plant are called "palma Christi" or "Christ's hands" because of their remarkable healing properties. The seeds are poisonous, however, so do warn your children to stay away from them.

CULTIVATION
The castor oil plant is a perennial shrub that grows to between 60 cm and 3 m. It likes full sun and thrives in any type of soil. It is grown from seed. Dig the soil over deeply in spring, add a spadeful of compost and plant two or three seeds about 60 cm apart. Cover with leaf mould and water well. Within a week the shoots will appear, and they will grow vigorously all summer. They may be struck down by frost but if the root is protected they will often send up new leaf shoots in spring.

USES
Domestic
☐ Sprinkle castor oil seeds at the entrances of mole burrows and the moles will abandon them.
☐ Castor oil is excellent for treating mange and skin ailments in dogs.

Medicinal
☐ The best-known medicinal use of castor oil is in the form of the famous oil, which is a purge. The warmed oil can also be applied to bruises and if rubbed into the scalp prior to shampooing helps prevent falling hair and aids hair growth. It can also be applied to the skin to relieve ringworm and mange. Take 2 parts castor oil and one part vinegar, mix together and warm, then rub into the troubled area night and morning.
☐ The oil can also be used to treat sore throats, swollen glands, mumps and stiff necks. Soak a piece of cloth in a cup of castor oil to which 10 drops of lavender oil and 2 sprays of rosemary oil have been added. Spread the cloth out in a shallow pan and place in a warm oven. Wring out the cloth and apply as hot as can be tolerated to the throat. Keep in place overnight with a lightly bound crêpe bandage.
☐ Castor oil leaves provide a pick-me-up for tired, aching feet. Warm a leaf or two in hot water, bind them around your feet with a warm towel and rest.
☐ The leaf is used for treating warts and tumours and as a drawing poultice for wounds and sores. The oil also helps remove blemishes and moles if rubbed onto the affected area daily.
☐ The juice from the stem is an effective toothache remedy. Pieces are chewed and then spat out, because if swallowed it is a powerful purge.
☐ In Zimbabwe the skin of the bark is used for stitching up wounds as well as a dressing for wounds and sores.
☐ NOTE: The seeds of the castor oil plant are poisonous if eaten.

CATNIP/KATTEKRUID

Nepeta mussinii, N. cataria
Family: Labiatae

Catnip (N. mussini)

Catnip, also known as catmint, is thought to be called after the Roman town Nepeti, where it was once extensively cultivated. It was once widely used as a seasoning and for medicinal purposes, but is less common today. Its leaves are also said to be mildly hallucinogenic when smoked. It is very attractive, but as its common name suggests it is much liked by cats, who tend to roll in the plants and eat the leaves. The smaller variety, N. Mussinii, is not so irresistible to cats and produces attractive bluish flowers. It's especially suitable for borders.

CULTIVATION

Catnip is a hardy herbaceous perennial.

Conditions: Can be grown in any soil, but likes sun or partial shade.

Propagation: By seed or cuttings. Take cuttings at any time of the year; keep cool and damp until well rooted. Protect with mesh to keep cats away. Once seeds have come up thin or transplant to 30 cm apart. *N. musinii* often branches and sends roots into the soil. If clipped away from the mother plant and allowed to establish, these new plants can later be transplanted.

Containers: *N. mussinii* is suitable for window boxes or hanging baskets, and can withstand baking sun on a patio.

Size: Grows to a height of 15 to 30 cm. *N. cataria* grows to between 30 and 50 cm.

Harvesting: The leaves can be picked when young, and the whole plant can be preserved by drying.

Dos and don'ts: Catnip will attract bees and butterflies (as well as cats!) to your garden. Do plant it near vegetables as it deters certain beetles. *N. musinii* produces a froth of palest mauve, blue and grey that sets off pink roses beautifully, so it makes an ideal edging for roses. Aphids can't stand it!

USES

Domestic

☐ Because cats love the smell of catnip the leaves can be dried and stuffed into little toys for them.

☐ The smell of catnip repels rats, and it makes a superb insect repelling spray.

Medicinal

☐ Catnip can be used to combat varicose veins. Make a mild tea by pouring 2 l of boiling water over a cup of leaves and flowers, let it stand for 15 minutes and then strain. Wring out cloths in this liquid and apply to the veins – hold in place for 30 minutes. Repeat three days running.

☐ The leaf and flowering top are rich in vitamin C. They can be made into an infusion to relieve colds and fevers; the plant induces sleep and perspiration without increasing body temperature. The standard brew is a cup of boiling water poured over a quarter cup of leaves and flowers. Strain and sweeten with honey.

☐ An infusion of catnip can be used to treat restlessness, colic and even bedwetting in children. Steep a sprig of catnip the size of an adult's thumb, together with a thumb-sized sprig of marjoram, in half a cup of boiling water. Stand for 5 minutes and strain. Sweeten with honey and give in small sips before the child goes to sleep.

☐ Catnip can be used to relieve pain associated with menstruation and digestion. Infuse 2 thumb-sized sprigs in one cup of boiling water, stand for 5 minutes and strain. Take one to three teaspoons before meals, or sip half a cup of standard brew twice during the day.

Culinary

☐ Catnip leaves can be rubbed on meat to flavour before cooking.

☐ The young shoots can be used as a salad vegetable, but in small quantities only as they have a very strong flavour.

CELERY/SELDERY
Apium graveolens
Family: Umbelliferae

This is a very well-known and popular herb, although it is usually thought of as a vegetable. Wild celery was used until the plant was domesticated in Italy in the 17th century. The Romans were partial to its taste. It is particularly versatile as the whole plant, from the leaves to the root, can be eaten, and it can be used in salads and hot dishes. Celery also has several medicinal uses. Celeriac tastes similar to celery but its leaves are coarser and it has a fleshy root and is superb in soups.

CULTIVATION
Celery is a biennial plant.

Conditions: Likes a moist, friable soil and a sunny position.

Propagation: Seeds can be sown in autumn, in boxes under cover or shallow drills. Cover them slightly with fine compost mixed with sand, followed by a light layer of fallen autumn leaves to protect in winter. Or sow in spring and cover the seeds with hessian to keep the soil moist. Where the plants come up too thickly, thin them by transplanting when they are not too big. Water well every three days and pile compost and sand around the base of the plant to assist in blanching the stems. Allow one or two plants to go to seed and collect the seed as soon as it is ripe. Store it in airtight bottles. Celery withstands the winter cold, so have seedlings at hand at all times to carry you through the seasons.

Size: Celery grows to a height of 20-50 cm.

Harvesting: For drying pull up plants that are going into the flowering stage, or pick off the outside leaves all through the year.

Dos and don'ts: Do plant celery near leeks as it benefits from their presence. Tomatoes and bush beans also make good neighbours for celery.

USES
Domestic
☐ Celery is an excellent compost maker. It helps to quickly break down the compost and yellowing or straggly leaves, flowering stalks, etc., can be layered between lawn clippings to break them down quickly.

Cosmetic
☐ An infusion of celery leaves applied with cotton wool makes an excellent cleanser for oily skin. Pour 2 cups boiling water over a cup of leaves, stand until lukewarm and then strain. A cup of the brew can be added to the rinsing water for oily hair.

Medicinal
☐ Fresh celery in the daily salad can be used to treat excess weight, rheumatism and nerves, and is an excellent tonic and stimulant. It also relieves flatulence.

☐ Celery seed or leaves, made into a tea, are a very effective diuretic. Make by adding 1 tsp of celery seed to 2 cups of boiling water, stand until lukewarm and then strain. Take once or twice a day. Alternatively, pour a cup of boiling water over a quarter cup of fresh leaves and stand for five minutes. Strain and take once a day for no more than 7 days. Allow a time lapse and then continue.

Culinary
☐ Besides its fresh uses, celery can also be cut and dried. Plants going into their flowering stage can be pulled up and dried in the shade on wire racks or on newspaper. Turn daily. Once dry they can be crumbled or chopped up for easier storage and then used in soups and stews or bouquet garnis.

☐ Celery is an excellent addition to soups, stews and sauces. Its flavour combines well with most vegetables.

☐ Celery seeds may be used to flavour savoury dishes and also in salad dressings as it cuts down on salt intake.

CHAMOMILE/KAMILLE
Matricaria recutita
Family: Compositae

Also known as German chamomile, this is one of the many varieties of chamomile (also spelt camomile). The plant has tall stems and small scented flowers consisting of yellow and white florets 15 mm to 3 cm wide, borne singly. The plant is indigenous to Europe and has been used there for centuries for medicinal purposes. The Egyptians dedicated chamomile to the sun and worshipped it for its incredible healing properties.

CULTIVATION

Chamomile is a short-lived annual plant that seeds itself every spring, sometimes twice in a good, moist season. It is very undemanding on the soil.

Conditions: Chamomile likes partial shade and light, well-drained soil.

Propagation: From seed. Sow seeds in sand-filled trays, pressing down well and covering with a fine layer of sand. Keep fairly moist until the seedlings are big enough to be handled. Plant out into well-dug and well composted light soil, in partial sunshine, about 20 cm apart, and keep well watered. Chamomile needs coolness and moisture to do well.

Size: Grows up to 40 cm.

Harvesting: The leaves can be picked at any time. The flowers should be gathered when they are fully open.

Dos and don'ts: Do plant chamomile near onions – at a rate of one chamomile plant to every 4 m of onions. Pick the flowers frequently to prolong its brief spring life.

Chamomile is an excellent companion for most plants – it is known as the "plant doctor."

USES

Domestic

☐ The flowers and leaves can be used to make potpourri and herb pillows.

☐ Chamomile tea is one of the most popular herbal teas and makes a particularly relaxing bedtime drink. It can be made by steeping a dessertspoonful of dried or fresh blossoms in a litre of boiling water, allowing it to stand for 10 minutes; strain and mix with honey.

☐ Chamomile tea without the honey can be used as a tonic spray for ailing plants. Soak two handfuls of flowers in 1 litre of boiling water overnight, then strain and spray.

Cosmetic

☐ The flower can be used in a facial steam infusion or as a cooled preparation to soak the hands to soften and whiten the skin. Boil a cup of flowers in 1 *l* of water to make the mixture.

☐ A tea bag eye compress can be made with an infusion of the flowers to reduce inflammation and dark shadows.

☐ Add an infusion of the flowers to a bath for a relaxing effect.

☐ Boil 2 cups of flowers for 20 minutes in 2 *l* of water and use the strained water regularly as a rinse to lighten and condition fair hair. It keeps well in the fridge.

Medicinal

☐ The flowers can be infused to make a brew with an excellent tonic and sedative effect. It is particularly effective if given to troubled infants. It can also be used to make a compress to treat wounds and eczema. Place 250 ml of leaves and blossom in 570 ml of boiling water to make an infusion. Stand for 20 minutes and strain, and take half a cup three times a day.

☐ Pour an infusion of chamomile flowers into the bath to relieve sunburn.

Culinary

☐ Chamomile tea can be added to granadilla juice and chilled for a relaxing cool drink. Add the tea to jellies and fruit drinks, or serve on its own as an after-dinner drink for indigestion!

CHERVIL/KERWEL
Anthriscus cerefolium
Family: Umbelliferae

Chervil is a useful and versatile culinary herb with a delicate flavour, belonging to the carrot family. It has been used medicinally since at least Roman times. Chervil is a pretty, fernlike plant.

CULTIVATION
Chervil is a delicate annual (sometimes biennial) plant.
Conditions: Chervil likes light shade in summer; it runs to seed quickly when it is very hot. The soil it is grown in should be light, well drained and cool.
Propagation: In spring from seed, which germinates quickly. Scatter the seeds on soil and press them in lightly. If left to self-seed, the plant will provide two crops a year. Thin the seedlings to 20 cm apart – transplant only on a cool day if necessary.

Size: The mature plant can reach between 30 and 46 cm in height.
Harvesting: Remove the leaves before flowering, when the plant is about 10 cm tall. It is usually ready for cutting 6-8 weeks after sowing.
Dos and don'ts: Do grow chervil under vines or fruit trees to protect it from the harsh sun. Do grow chervil near radishes as they encourage its growth.

USES
Domestic
☐ Crushed chervil leaves rubbed on window sills and kitchen counters help to keep flies away. Added to fresh basil leaves they are good for rubbing into furniture to keep flies out and mosquitoes at bay.

Cosmetic
☐ The leaves of chervil can be used in an infusion or face mask to cleanse and condition the skin.

Medicinal
☐ The leaf is full of vitamin C, carotene and certain minerals and can be eaten in raw form added to salads, etc.
☐ An infusion of chervil leaves can be made to stimulate digestion and relieve disorders of the circulation, liver complaints and catarrh.
☐ Chervil is a blood cleanser and effective rheumatic and kidney treatment. The standard brew can be made by pouring a cup of boiling water over a quarter cup of fresh leaves. Stand for five minutes then strain.

Culinary
☐ Chervil is one of the ingredients of *fines herbes* and is indispensable in gourmet cooking. It can be used as a replacement for parsley.
☐ Chervil leaf can be used in soups, salads, sauces, vegetables, fish, chicken and egg dishes. Add it near the end of cooking. It combines well with other herbs.
☐ Use the stem of chervil raw and chopped in salads, and cooked in casseroles and soups.
☐ Chervil is a versatile and attractive garnish when used in the same way as parsley.

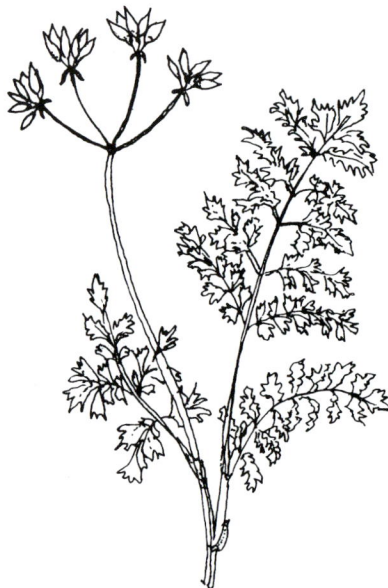

CHICKWEED/SEWESTER/ MIERGRAS/MUGGIEGRAS

Stellaria media
Family: Caryophyllaceae

This plant is also known as the starflower. Native to Europe, it was introduced to South Africa in the 1700s, probably transported in horses' bedding and hay. It now appears as a weed in gardens everywhere. As its name suggests, chickens love eating the leaves, and its seed and leaves are also used as a food for caged birds.

CULTIVATION

Chickweed is a vigorous creeping annual with tiny oval leaves and small star-shaped white flowers. It grows easily in almost any soil, but prefers moist places. It usually grows as a weed, but tiny seedlings can be transplanted carefully. It can be harvested at any time. Chickweed is tender and fragile and doesn't like the soil around it to be disturbed.

USES

Domestic

☐ Give fresh chickweed leaves to poultry. Save the seeds and leaves for caged birds. Whenever there is an abundance, add to compost – it is rich in nitrogen.

Cosmetic

☐ Chickweed has antiseptic qualities and can be made into a mild lotion and dabbed onto spotty and problem skins.
☐ Chickweed is also an excellent slimming herb. Made as a standard brew it is to be taken once or twice a week.

Medicinal

☐ Chickweed has been used for a long time in South Africa to treat haemorrhoids, blood diseases, eczema and other disorders.
☐ Fresh chickweed leaves, if added to a poultice, will help relieve inflammation and bring a boil to a head. A brew can also be made from the leaves and stems and applied to skin and eye eruptions.
☐ Chickweed is used homeopathically in the treatment of rheumatism.
☐ A decoction of the whole plant can be made to treat constipation and piles. It can also be applied to eczema and psoriasis.
☐ Chickweed tea aids indigestion and soothes the digestive tract. To make the tea, add a quarter cup of chickweed to a cup of boiling water. Stand for 5 minutes and strain. When cooled, this same tea can be used as a lotion for skin ailments, as described above.

Culinary

☐ Chickweed leaves are high in vitamin C and phosphorus and can be added to salads or cooked as a vegetable with spinach.
☐ Add chickweed leaves to soups and stews in the last few minutes of cooking time. Use it in salads – it is pleasant tasting and pretty as a garnish.
☐ The Tswana people gather young chickweed shoots and add potatoes and onions to make a type of spinach dish. It is believed to give them strong blood.

CHICORY/SIGOREI
Chichorium intybus
Family: Compositae

Chicory has grown wild throughout Europe for many centuries, and it has been harvested and used at least since ancient Egyptian times for medical purposes. Its traditional uses were to treat liver and gallbladder complaints. Its most familiar use nowadays is in the form of the roasted ground root which is added to instant coffee or used as a coffee substitute itself. Chicory has beautiful blue flowers with a multitude of uses. Folklore has it that they are the transformed eyes of a girl weeping for her lost lover. There is a wild variety with serrated leaves and bright blue flowers which is a roadside delight! Chicory is very bitter, although the whole plant is quite edible.

CULTIVATION
Chicory is a perennial plant.
Conditions: Chicory likes deep, rich soil, and a sunny situation.
Propagation: By seed. Sow in sand trays and cover with a piece of glass until the seedlings are strong. Keep well watered at all times. Plant out into a well-prepared bed 30 cm apart and keep shaded for a day or two. In very hot weather the plant runs to seed so it's best to sow seeds in March for planting out in winter.

Size: Grows up to 120 cm in height, including flowering head.
Harvesting: Pick the leaves when young and flowers in midsummer. Dig up roots in the first autumn.
Dos and don'ts: Chicory is an excellent compost maker. Grow extra plants and cut them back lavishly for the compost heap. The inclusion of chicory in the compost heap generates double the compost in half the time! Do plant chicory leaves near beans, spinach and pumpkins. It also makes an excellent companion for mealies, and a superb fodder plant.

USES
Domestic
☐ The leaves and flowering stems yield a blue dye when boiled.

Medicinal
☐ Chicory is rich in vitamins and minerals which give it a diuretic and tonic effect. The whole plant has tonic properties.
☐ Make a chicory tea by adding half a cup of leaves and flowers to 500 ml boiling water. Allow to stand for five minutes and then strain. Store in the fridge and take a small wineglass full three times a day in cases of jaundice, anaemia, weak sight, infertility and liver disorders. Include a little chicory in the diet too, it is a tonic herb.
☐ A poultice of boiled flowers and leaves is an excellent remedy for inflammations, boils and septic areas.

Culinary
☐ Chicory can be used as a vegetable if blanched, a process which reduces the extreme bitterness of the plant. The favourite variety is witloof. To blanche your own, dig out several plants 4-6 months after planting seedlings, then cut off the foliage and stand the roots close together in a deep box or pot. Cover with 15 cm of light, sandy soil, press down lightly and keep moist, but do not overwater. Store in a cool, dark shed. As they grow the young leaves become elongated and blanched, and the plant should resemble a pale elongated lettuce. If exposed to light the leaves become very green and bitter. The plants are ready for lifting when the white leaves (chicons) appear. Blanched chicory is delicious with a cheese sauce.
☐ If you want to use the unblanched plant, use the young leaves only. They can be added in moderation to salads, as can the decorative blue flowers.
☐ Chicory protects the liver against excessive coffee drinking. Mince well-washed roots, spread on baking trays and place in a low oven overnight. Grind in a coffee grinder and store in airtight bottles. Add to coffee or use on its own.

CHIVE/GRASUI

Allium tuberosum, A. schoenoprasum
Family: Liliaceae

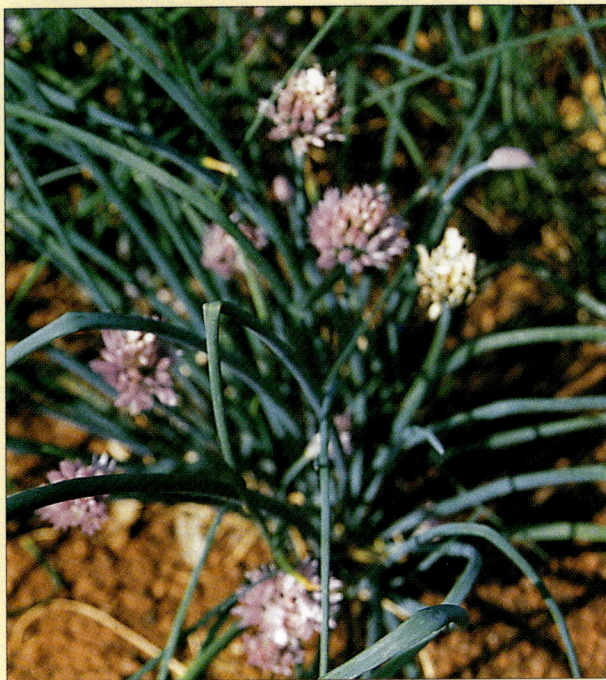

Chives belong to the same family as onions and garlic, and they are also extremely useful in the kitchen. A. tuberosum, the white-flowered garlic chive, has a distinctive garlicky flavour and grows as prolifically as A. schoenoprasum, which has mauvy-pink flowers. A. tuberosum, like chives, dies down in winter. The Chinese chive is a larger-leafed variety which does not die down in the winter. It has a fresh onion-garlic flavour and is superb in stir fries. It has a large head of white flowers. An indigenous variety of garlic chive is Tulbaghia alliacea. It has edible flowers which are delicious in salads. Another member of the Tulbaghia group, T. violacea or wild garlic, is also a wonderful salad ingredient. All of these grow as easily as members of the onion family. Chives are indigenous to Europe and North America, but have been cultivated since the middle ages.

CULTIVATION

Chives are perennials

Conditions: They like fairly rich soil and sun, but can withstand partial shade.

Propagation: Seeds can be sown in trays at any time except May-July. Keep them under glass until 1 or 2 cm high and harden off by exposing to a little sun daily. Plant out 20 cm apart when big enough to handle. Clumps will form lasting 4 to 5 years; they can be redivided. Garlic chives are also unfussy growers.

Size: Grows to a height of between 15 and 30 cm.

Harvesting: The flowering heads appear in summer and can be picked for salads, while the more mature flowers can be made into a delicious vinegar. Chives can be dried, but are far more delicious fresh.

Dos and don'ts: Do plant chives if you want to attract bees to your garden.

USES

Medicinal

☐ Chives have a blood cleansing, tonic effect and improve the appetite. They also help ward off colds and flu.

Culinary

☐ Chives can be used to flavour almost any savoury dish. They are one of the ingredients of *fines herbes*. Add chopped, fresh chives to dishes such as stews and soups in the last five minutes of cooking.

☐ Chives are particularly delicious with egg and cheese dishes and cream cheese.

☐ Use chive flowers in salads and to make flavoured vinegar.

Tulbaghia violacea

COLUMBINE/AKELEI

Aquilegia vulgaris
Family: Ranunculaceae

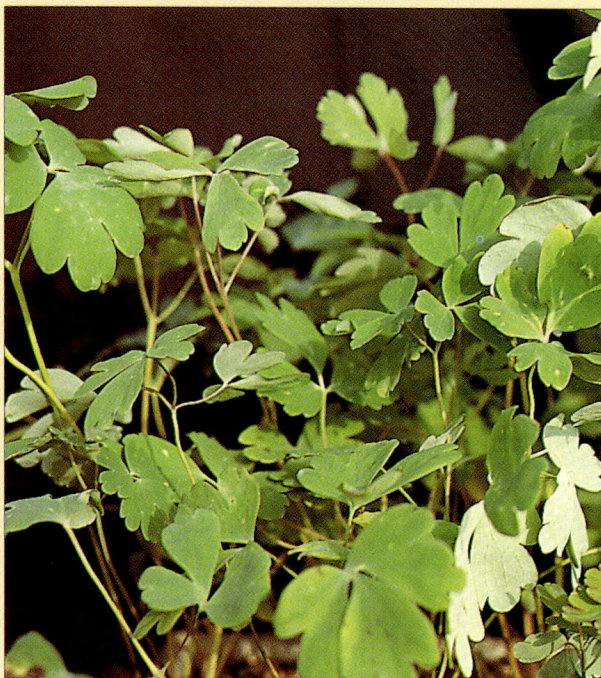

The name "columbine" derives from the Latin word "columba" meaning "dove," because the curved shape of the flower's spurs was thought to resemble the claws of a dove. In the middle ages it was called "aquilinae," from the Latin "aquila" or "eagle," again because of the similarity between the spurs and the shape of a bird of prey's claws. In the 17th century it was used to relieve scurvy and to combat hysteria and sleeplessness. It is still used in homeopathic remedies for menstrual problems, insomnia and nerves. The plant is poisonous, however, so it should be used only under the guidance of a homeopathic doctor. The seed is extremely poisonous and may be fatal if swallowed by a child. The roots, leaves and flowers all have antiseptic, astringent and sedative properties, but only the root may be used externally (for the treatment of ulcers).

Columbine has thin, upright stems topped by drooping flowers in spring and summer. It is now available in a variety of colours, though the old-fashioned columbine favoured blue, pink and white. Although it is no longer widely used for medicinal purposes it makes a graceful and attractive addition to the garden. It will also attract bees.

CULTIVATION

Columbine is a perennial plant that likes a rich, well-drained soil and partial shade. It grows up to 60 cm in height and may be propagated by seeds or by division. Sow the seeds in trays, keeping them moist and under glass until they germinate. Keep seedlings shaded and well watered until they are strong enough to be handled. Plant them in partial shade in well-dug, rich soil to which several spadefuls of compost have been added. Keep well watered until they are established, then water once a week. Separate in spring if the clump grows too large. Dig in a spade of compost around each plant in spring.

USES
Medicinal

☐ To treat an ulcer, make a columbine compress. Crush a cup of the roots, stems and leaves of columbine together with a cup of the leaves and a few pieces of the root of the comfrey plant. Mix in a little warm water. Carefully bathe the ulcerated area with thyme or comfrey lotion and apply the mixture to it with thin gauze. Bind the area with a crêpe bandage for about half an hour. Remove and re-apply as advised by a doctor.

COMFREY/SMEERWORTEL

Symphytum officinale
Family: Boraginaceae

Comfrey is also known as "knit-bone," a reference to its capacity to aid in the healing of bones. It also has a multitude of other medicinal uses, and is a real miracle-worker among herbs. It is native to Europe and Asia but grows well in many parts of the world. Comfrey generally grows well in South Africa but as it likes water it does not do well in times of drought. It is growing in importance as an animal feed, and is a particularly rich source of protein. Comfrey reached the height of its popularity as a healing herb in the 16th century.

CULTIVATION

Conditions: Likes sun or partial shade and an average soil, but requires moisture to grow really well.
Propagation: Division, pieces of root. Keep root or division moist until well established; manure soil well.
Size: Grows to 30 to 60 cm.
Harvesting: Fresh leaves can be picked any time; leaves can be dried for winter use, then stored in airtight glass bottles or made into an oil (see medicinal uses). Roots may be dug up in autumn or winter, cleaned and dried.
Dos and don'ts: Comfrey is ideal for badly drained areas or swampy ground. Do put unwanted or used comfrey leaves on the compost heap; they break down quickly and easily and add nourishing minerals to the compost. Comfrey will attract bees to your garden. Comfrey is beneficial to all surrounding plants as it brings up rich trace elements and provides moisture, shade and shelter to plants grown nearby.

USES

Domestic

☐ The leaves may be soaked in water for four weeks to make an excellent fertiliser for tomatoes and potatoes. Leaves can also be used chopped as a mulch, but wait at least 48 hours after picking.
☐ The fresh leaves may be boiled to produce a rich golden fabric dye.

Cosmetic

☐ Add the leaf and root of comfrey to baths and lotions to soften the skin.

Medicinal

☐ Contact your doctor before taking comfrey internally. Recent medical research has indicated that comfrey may damage the liver.
☐ Comfrey was once the main herb used in the treatment of fractures. It contains allantoin, which helps in healing, and the pounded root forms a mucilaginous mass which can be bound over the fracture; as it dries it hardens and helps keep the bone in place.
☐ Comfrey is used to treat ulcers, tuberculosis, pneumonia, ruptures, burns and bruises. For bruises, swellings and sprains chop three or four comfrey leaves finely, soften in hot water and apply to the affected area on a square of lint. Cover with plastic and bandage in place. For internal use a tablespoon of chopped comfrey can be added to a cup of boiling water. Stand for 5 minutes only, then strain. Do not take more than 1 cup a day, and limit it to twice a week.
☐ For skin irritations make a comfrey oil. Pick clean, dry leaves and cut into 25 mm squares. Pack into a clean, dark jar and cover with a good oil. Apply a screw-top lid; do not open for two years. A quicker method is to warm equal quantities of chopped comfrey and aqueous cream for 20 minutes, strain into sterilised jars.
☐ Rub the juice of fresh comfrey leaves on the skin to soothe insect bites and stings and to repel insects.
☐ Comfrey root can be used to make a remedy for gout. Boil three tablespoons of chopped, well washed root in four cups of water for 20 minutes. Steep, then strain and bottle. Store in fridge; take one small wineglassful three times a day for a maximum of three days running. Miss 2 days and continue for no more than 10 days.

Culinary

☐ Chop the young leaves finely and use in salads, soups and stews.
☐ The young leaves can be coated in batter, fried in oil and served with salt and pepper.
☐ The stem can be blanched and cooked like asparagus. Do not eat more than once weekly.

CORIANDER/KOLJANDER
Coriandrum sativum
Family: Umbelliferae

Coriander has been cultivated for at least 3 000 years and has many culinary and medicinal uses. It was widely used throughout the ancient world and introduced to northern Europe by the Romans, who used it as a meat preservative. It was also traditionally used in love potions and aphrodisiacs. The plant smells strongly, and in fact the name derives from the Greek word "koris," meaning "bedbug," as it has a similar smell. The seed is the part most used for culinary purposes, and is present in ground form in most commercially produced curry powders.

CULTIVATION

Coriander is a hardy annual with small white or pale mauve flowers and is one of the most attractive members of the *Umbelliferae* family.

Conditions: It likes full sun and rich, light soil. Coriander is easy to grow.

Propagation: Can be sown from seed in autumn in moderate climates, or in early spring. Sow in spring in the position where you want it to grow. Make a shallow drill in light, well-tilled soil and sow seeds 15-20 cm apart. Cover them with sand and a layer of compost to retain the moisture. Cover with hessian and keep damp until the seedlings are well established. Then harden them off by exposing to full sunlight initially for two hours a day, increasing by two hours daily until they can withstand the elements. You can sow seeds every fortnight to ensure a continuous crop.

Containers: It can be placed in a large pot on a veran-dah or patio in the sun, and grown in such a position it is very useful as you can easily pick a sprig if you need one for cooking. If using it as a container plant, however, beware that it can become very straggly if you wait for the seed heads to dry.

Size: Grows up to 60 cm.

Harvesting: Young leaves can be picked at any time, but the seeds should be collected when they turn brown and before they drop.

Dos and don'ts: Don't grow coriander next to fennel, as it inhibits seed formation in fennel. Do grow coriander next to aniseed, as it seems to speed up the aniseed's growth. Coriander flowers will attract bees.

USES

Domestic
☐ Coriander makes a superb insect repelling spray. Add half a bucket of leaves, flowers and stems to half a bucket of mixed khakibos leaves, basil or southernwood leaves and pour over this one bucket of boiling water. Stand overnight, then strain and add two cups of soap powder.
☐ Coriander seed can be added to potpourri.

Cosmetic
☐ Coriander can be used to make a soothing face pack for oily, spotty skin. Mix half a cup of coriander flowers with a cup of oats and two cups of warm water. Leave overnight in a thermos and apply to skin for 10 minutes. Rinse off with tepid water.

Medicinal
☐ Coriander seed can be chewed or drunk in the form of an infusion as a digestive tonic. Place 2 teaspoons of seed in a cup of boiling water then stand and cool. Strain and drink a small quantity at frequent intervals.
☐ Essential oil of coriander can be added to rheumatic ointments, or the warmed, crushed seeds applied direct to the rheumatic area to relieve pain. Mix with warm water and spread on a cloth, then bind the cloth into place. It can also be used to prevent griping caused by other medication, taken as the above brew.

Culinary
☐ The seed is used in many dishes both sweet and savoury, including curries, chutneys, cakes, biscuits and marmalade. Seeds can also be added to soups and vegetable dishes, but use sparingly as they are strong-tasting.
☐ Coriander leaf can be used in salads, sauces and hot meat dishes or used as a garnish like parsley. The leaves are sometimes sold as "Chinese parsley," "cilantro" or "danya."
☐ The stem of coriander can be added to soups.
☐ Coriander root can be cooked as a vegetable.
☐ Coriander seeds can be used to make a delicious mixed spice. Add in equal quantities to cinnamon and nutmeg and a half quantity of cloves. Mix well.

DANDELION/PERDEBLOM
Taraxacum officinale
Family: Compositae

Dandelion, with its familiar puffball flowers, is commonly considered to be a weed, but it has excellent medicinal qualities. Its name is derived from the French "dents de lion," meaning "the teeth of the lion," from their jagged shape. It is indigenous to Europe and Asia but is found wild in many other places as well. It has been used as a medicine and food since the 13th century.

CULTIVATION

The dandelion is a common weed, but as it can easily be confused with other weeds, take care when picking it. It grows all year round and is common on lawns. Dandelion withstands frost well. It seeds itself everywhere and benefits from picking, so pick the flowers frequently.

Dos and don'ts: Dandelion exhales a gas, ethylene, which inhibits the growth of plants nearby, but helps them to mature early. Dandelions grow well in combination with lucerne.

USES

Domestic
☐ Dandelion leaves are an excellent addition to compost as they hasten the breakdown of the compost and provide vital nourishment.

Cosmetic
☐ Dandelion contains a rich emollient that can be added to cleansers used for dry or mature skins.
☐ The milk of the stem is a quick pimple treatment.

Medicinal
☐ Dandelion is a very effective diuretic and is also valuable in treating liver complaints. The leaves have tonic and laxative effects, improve the digestion and strengthen tooth enamel. For diuretic purposes a tablespoon of dandelion root can be drawn in one cup of boiling water and drunk three times daily.
☐ The milky juice from dandelion stems and leaves can be applied to warts and blisters to remove them; it should be applied daily. If very diluted the juice can also be used to relieve sore and red eyes. Wipe it on the outside of the eyes.

Culinary
☐ Dandelion leaves are rich in vitamins and minerals and can be added raw to salads, but should be used sparingly as they have a bitter taste.
☐ Dried and powdered dandelion roots can be used as a coffee substitute, and for beer making.
☐ The flowers can be used to make a delicious dandelion wine that also has therapeutic effects.
☐ The entire plant can be used in soups, stews and vegetable dishes.

DOCK/WILDE SURING OF TONGBLAAR

Rumex obtusifolius
Family: Polygonaceae

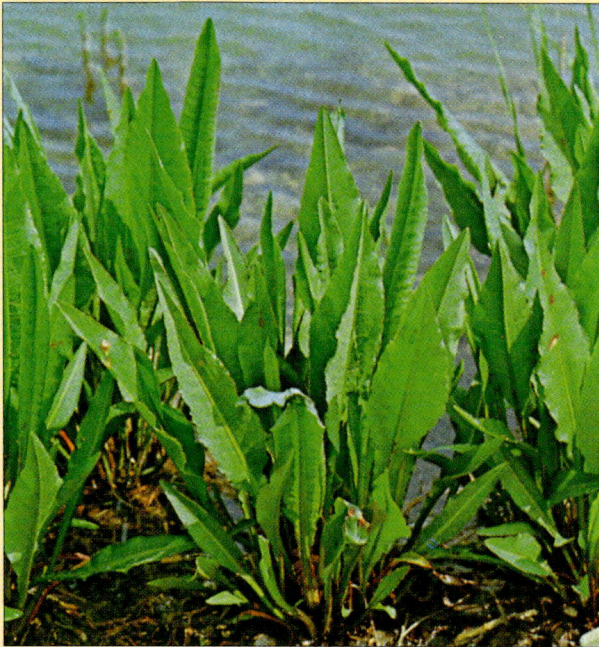

Dock is a close relative of sorrel and has a multitude of medicinal uses. Although native to Europe, it is now found in many sub-tropical as well as temperate countries, where it often grows as a weed. Hundreds of years ago dock was used to wrap butter when it was taken to market, and fresh dock leaves can be placed in butter dishes to keep the butter fresh.

CULTIVATION

Dock grows wild as a weed, often in cultivated fields and along furrows. It is easily recognised by its attractive tall brown seed heads and big leaves, which may be harvested at any time of the year.

USES

Domestic

☐ Certain black people use a decoction of dock to treat anthrax, often combining it with galbos (*Teucrium africanum*).

Medicinal

☐ Crushed dock leaves are excellent for soothing red, sunburnt skin – made into a lotion, or crushed and applied to the skin. It also soothes skin irritations caused by rashes, mosquito bites and stinging nettles.

☐ Dock contains tannins, resins, salts, volatile oils, starches and thiamine. It has astringent and purgative properties and is used as a tonic laxative and for skin complaints.

☐ Dock leaves can be applied to ringworm, scabies and urticaria. The Tswana warm dock leaves to dress swollen breasts during lactation, and also pound and pulp the leaves for use as a pile treatment.

☐ The dried rhizome of the dock plant was once used to purify the blood and treat skin diseases, as well as a general tonic.

☐ Powdered, dried root of dock mixed with warm water is used as a gargle to treat laryngitis, and as a mouthwash. It is also effective against gingivitis. The mixture is 2 teaspoons of crushed root boiled in 2 cups of water for 15 minutes then strained.

Culinary

☐ Dock leaves may be stuffed to make a delicious savoury dish. The stuffing consists of rice, bacon, mushrooms and onion, which is lightly fried and then rolled in blanched dock leaves and served warm. Young leaves are preferable as they are more tender.

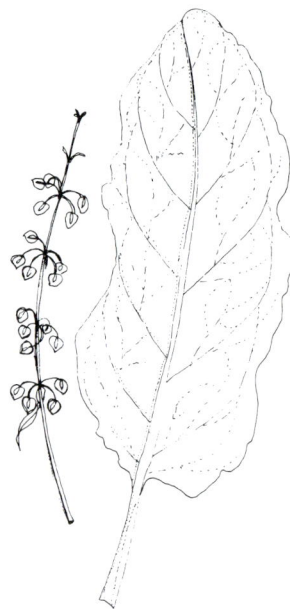

ELDER/VLIERBOOM
Sambucus nigra
Family: Caprifoliaceae

The elder tree is the source of elderberries, and it grows wild in many countries, including some parts of South Africa. It is a very useful plant and almost every part of it has medicinal or culinary value. The berries are commercially important in jams and fruit juices. In ancient times the elder tree was accorded magical properties, and was said to keep witches away. The elder has been used at least since ancient Egyptian times. It is native to Asia, Europe and the British Isles.

CULTIVATION
Elder is a perennial, deciduous small tree or large shrub with small umbrels of creamy-white flowers and spreading branches with serrated leaves.

Conditions: Elders tolerate most soil, and thrive in dry areas. They also need full sun.

Propagation: By runners or cuttings. To check the invading roots, which send up vigorous small trees, line the hole with thick plastic around the sides. fill with topsoil and compost and then plant the tree; firm well and keep watered until new growth is started. In frosty areas trim back neatly in winter; the cut branches can be pressed into wet sand to start new trees.

Size: 90 cm to 3,6 m.

Harvesting: Pick the flowers all through summer, but leave some for berries. In South Africa's heat the berries don't set abundantly and are much loved by birds, but by autumn are ready for picking.

Dos and don'ts: Do plant elders as a hedge. Elders can be clipped into a pleasing umbrella shape and make a pretty specimen tree in a small garden. Elders benefit from regular pruning.

USES
Domestic
☐ An infusion of elder leaves can be wiped over arms and legs to keep mosquitoes at bay. Tuck a spray into your garden hat to keep insects away.

☐ Elder leaves added to compost make a superb nutrient. Add all the prunings to the compost heap.

Cosmetic
☐ An infusion of elder flowers is good for the skin, especially sallow and older skins. It is said to smooth wrinkles and fade freckles. Make it by pouring a litre of boiling water over 2 cups of elder flowers. Stand until cool, strain and soak a cotton wool pad in the liquid.

Medicinal
☐ The flowers can be infused to treat colds. They are also used in an ointment to treat burns. The berries are used to make cough mixture.

☐ Ointment made from the leaves is used to relieve bruises, sprains and chilblains. Make it by heating 1 part fresh leaves with 2 parts petroleum jelly until the leaves become crisp. Strain before use.

☐ Elderflower tea is effective against hangovers. Make it by pouring a cup of boiling water over a quarter cup of elder flowers. Stand for 5 minutes and strain.

☐ Elder root, soaked in water, is good for kidney complaints. Pour 2 litres of warm water over 1 cup of chopped, clean roots. Take half a cup four times a day.

☐ Dried and powdered elder bark is used to prepare a wine that combats epileptic fits. Make it by drying the inner bark of old branches and stems and steeping 12,5 ml of this bark in a small glass of red or white wine. A dose taken nightly in the epileptic's quiet periods is beneficial and when a fit is expected a wineglass full can be taken every 20 minutes. It is advisable to consult your doctor first.

☐ An infusion of 750 ml leaves to a litre of water, boiled for 20 minutes and then strained, may be applied when cool to nappy rash and eczema. If equal quantities of scented geranium leaves and 2-4 cloves of garlic are added to the same brew, it makes a potent remedy for bites, itches, rashes and ringworm. Apply frequently.

☐ The juice of the ripe berries can be applied directly to burns to give relief.

Culinary
☐ Elderberries are rich in vitamin C and make delicious jam, syrup, fruit juice and wine.

☐ Elder flowers can be added to pancakes, cakes, creams and custards. In fact the whole flower can be dipped into batter and fried as a fritter, served with whipped cream, sugar and cinnamon.

☐ Elder buds can be added to pickles and fruit salads.

EVENING PRIMROSE/ REUSE AANDBLOMMETJIE

Oenothera biennis
Family: Onagraceae

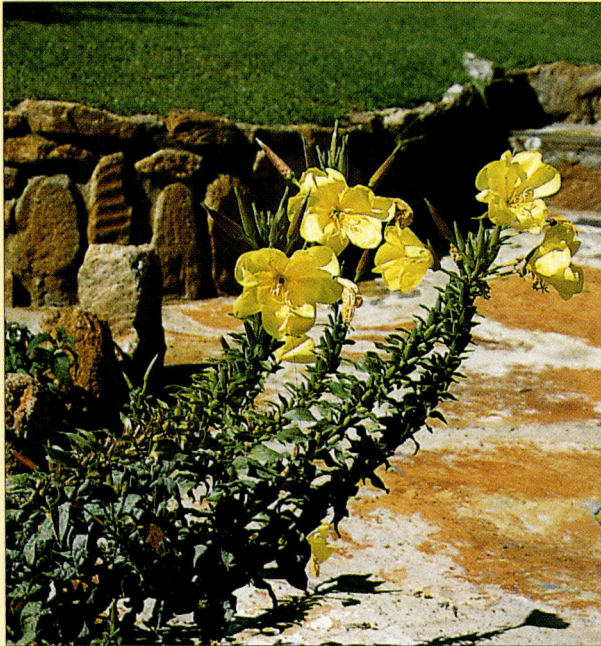

As its name suggests, the evening primrose has the delightful habit of opening its yellow blooms at night, when its sweet scent is at its best. Evening primrose has become a household name in the past few years, largely because of its increasing medical importance. The seeds contain the rare gamma-linoleic acid and extracts are used to alleviate pre-menstrual tension and other "female" complaints. Research is also being done on its effects on thrombosis and psoriasis, as well as its ability to control degenerative diseases like multiple sclerosis. Other areas of research include treatment for rheumatoid arthritis, Parkinson's disease, breast tumours, hyperactivity and schizoprenia!

CULTIVATION
Evening primrose is a biennial plant
Conditions: It likes sun and prefers well-drained soil.
Propagation: It can be grown from seed, planted 30 cm apart, and self-seeds in light soil.
Size: It grows to between 1 and 2m in height.
Dos and don'ts: Do not confuse this with the smaller roadside varieties, often also called *aandblommetjies.* The evening primrose grows to over a metre high in fields where there is a little moisture, or in ditches, vleis and on the edge of ploughed land.

USES
Domestic
☐ The leaves make an excellent foliar feed for pot plants and vegetables.
☐ Toss spent flowering heads onto the compost heap – the seedlings that come up can be transplanted or added to the compost where they will add valuable chorophyll and nitrogen.

Cosmetic
☐ The leaves and stems can be boiled in water to make a soothing astringent lotion for greasy, spotty skin. The same lotion is an excellent wash for eczema, psoriasis, rashes, insect bites, scrapes and grazes.
☐ To soften dry skin heat together a cup of chopped leaves, buds and stems and a cup of aqueous cream, remove from heat, strain and cool.
☐ The flowers can be crushed and applied to spots, rashes and itchy mosquito bites.

Medicinal
☐ Evening primrose is being tested for use in heart complaints (it is a natural anticoagulant), psoriasis, gastric irritations, high cholesterol, multiple sclerosis, high blood pressure, chest ailments and many other medical problems.

Culinary
☐ The flowers can be chopped and eaten in salads.
☐ The young leaves can be boiled and eaten like spinach.
☐ The roots, dug up in the second year before the plant sets seed, can be pickled and eaten with salads and savoury dishes.

FENNEL/VINKEL
Foeniculum vulgare, F. var *dulce*
Family: Umbelliferae

Fennel was one of the first plants to be cultivated by man, and it has always been highly valued, particularly for its culinary properties. It also has numerous medicinal uses, which were widely exploited by the Romans. The Anglo-Saxons believed that it could keep away evil.

Foeniculum vulgare is chiefly used as a flavouring, while F. var *dulce, or Florence fennel, is a delicious vegetable, known as "finocchio" in Italy. The entire fennel plant is edible.*

CULTIVATION
Fennel is a hardy herbaceous perennial, easily identified by its flat yellow flower clusters borne on stalks radiating from the main stem.

Conditions: Fennel is easy to grow but its position in the garden should be carefully chosen as it is a bad companion to certain other plants. It likes well-drained loamy soil and full sun.

Propagation: Fennel seeds itself readily and can be transplanted easily while still small. Plant the seedlings 50-60 cm apart and keep them moist for a few weeks until they are well established.

Size: Average of 60 cm, grows up to 150 cm in some areas, such as the Cape.

Harvesting: Stems and leaves can be picked as required. Collect the ripe seeds.

Dos and don'ts: Don't plant fennel near coriander, bush beans, cucumber, tomatoes, kohlrabi or caraway. Fennel suffers when planted near wormwood. Don't plant it near dill, either, or it will cross-pollinate with the dill. Fennel will attract butterflies to your garden.

USES
Domestic
☐ Fennel seeds are a useful fixative for potpourri. Crush and mix with powdered cinnamon and nutmeg.
☐ Fennel leaves added to compost make it friable.

Cosmetic
☐ Fennel can be used to make an eye bath. Mix 45 g chopped leaves with a litre of boiled water, stand for 5 minutes and then strain. This liquid can also be drunk as a tonic and is believed to aid memory, digestion and obesity, but do not take more than two cups daily for more than a week.
☐ Fennel seeds and leaves can be added to the boiling water used for steaming the face.

Medicinal
☐ Chewing fennel seeds sweetens the breath.
☐ The seed is antiseptic, and an infusion of 2 tsp finely crushed seeds in a cup of boiling water that has been left to stand for 10 minutes and then strained will help expel poisons from the body after a snake, dog or insect bite. Needless to say, this should not be the only treatment applied – especially in the case of snakebite!
☐ Fennel is a good digestive herb – a leaf or piece of stem can be chewed after big meals to prevent indigestion. A tea made with 1 tsp of bruised seeds to a cup of boiling water helps combat flatulence, colic and an overfull feeling. Alternatively, pour a cup of boiling water over a quarter cup of fresh fennel leaves, stand for five minutes and then strain.
☐ Fennel water in soups and stews aids weight loss. This brew can also be used for slimming purposes: 250 ml (1 cup) chopped leaves and stalk boiled in 750 ml (3 cups) of water for 6-10 minutes. Keep the pot covered. Cool and drink at intervals during the day. Do not exceed 2 cups a day for more than a week.
☐ When the seeds are chewed, or the herb is taken as a tea, fennel eases indigestion.

Culinary
Fennel has a strong flavour and does not blend well with other herbs, except for chives and parsley.
☐ The bulb of *F.* var *dulce* can be boiled and served with a cheese sauce. It is also delicious when finely shaved into salads.
☐ Finely chopped fennel leaves enhance the flavour of fish dishes and green beans.
☐ The young stems of *F. vulgare* can be chopped into salads or cooked and served like asparagus, but the stems must be cut before the flowers open. The chopped leaves can be mixed with cream cheese and sprinkled with lemon pepper to make a delicious dip.
☐ Fennel seeds can be used in pickles and sauces and for flavouring breads.
☐ When the fennel plants start to look tatty, cut the stems to use when grilling fish. Lay the fish on top of the stems and let the fragrance and flavour permeate the fish. Discard the stems after cooking the fish.

FENUGREEK/FENEGRIEK

Trigonella foenum-graecum
Family: Leguminosae

The Greeks, Romans and ancient Egyptians all cultivated fenugreek for its culinary and medicinal value. It was used especially for embalming. Fenugreek seed has been used in India for a very long time as an ingredient in curry powder. Fenugreek is an important fodder crop, and it is becoming commercially important in the field of medicine as it contains mucilage and the substance known as diosgenin, used in oral contraceptives and hormone preparations.

CULTIVATION

Fenugreek is a tender annual with slightly toothed 3-lobed small leaves and a small yellowish flower.

Conditions: It likes a sunny position and fertile, well drained soil, preferably alkaline.

Propagation: By seed, which can be bought from health shops. Thin the seedlings to about 10 cm apart, as fenugreek is difficult to transplant.

Containers: Fenugreek can be grown indoors on trays lined with wet cotton wool, or sprouted in a jar. It is the young plant that is most often used.

Size: Varies from 30 to 60 cm.

Harvesting: Pick the leaves when required. Gather the seeds when they ripen.

Dos and don'ts: Do plant fenugreek as a green crop for depleted soils. Dig the plants in once they reach maturity. Do plant it near tomatoes, beans and lettuce. It is a rewarding companion to squashes and cucumbers – if planted all round them it keeps insects away.

USES

Domestic
☐ The seeds can be boiled up to produce a yellow dye.

Cosmetic
☐ When infused the seed makes an excellent face wash for oily, problem skins. Pour 1 *l* of boiling water over half a cup of seed. Stand, cool and strain.
☐ The seed can be powdered and mixed with petroleum jelly to soothe chapped lips. It can also be soaked in water and added to home-made hand creams.

Medicinal
☐ Ground fenugreek seed can be made into a tea that is said to ease coughing and stomach disorders such as flatulence. It stimulates digestion and helps ensure a healthy milk flow in lactating women. It is also said to relieve fevers. Make this tea by stirring 1 teaspoonful of ground seed into a cup of boiling water. Let it stand until pleasantly warm, then sip slowly.
☐ A poultice of crushed seed, warmed in water, can be applied to inflammation, bruises and sciatica.

Culinary
☐ Fenugreek seed is used in curries. It is usually roasted and crushed before using for this purpose.
☐ The sprouts can be used in salads. When the plant is a little older it can be cooked as a vegetable with spinach or beans; it is especially tasty when added to curried dishes.

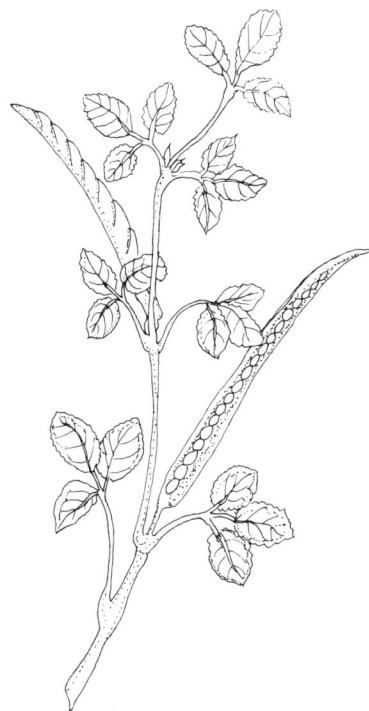

FEVERFEW/MOEDERKRUID
Chrysanthemum parthenium
Family: Compositae

It has long been known that feverfew has medicinal properties, especially the capacity to cure headaches and migraines, and modern research has shown that it even helps in arthritis. Its effectiveness in combating migraine may be because of its effect in reducing the smooth muscle spasms associated with this condition. The whole plant is strongly aromatic and repels insects.

CULTIVATION
Feverfew is a hardy biennial, sometimes perennial if the flowering head is cut off, and makes a very attractive garden plant.

Conditions: The plant prefers a sunny position, with dry, well-drained soil.

Propagation: Feverfew self-seeds well and the seeds can be sown in spring or autumn. Sow in boxes of river sand. Keep shaded and damp under a pane of glass until the seedlings are up. Then keep watered until they can be hardened off by exposing them to sunlight for periods of increasing length each day. Plant 30 cm apart in well-dug and composted soil. Stem cuttings may be taken in summer. Pull off lower small branches with a small "heel" and insert into sand, keeping moist until they root. Thin or transplant the seedlings to 30 cm apart.

Containers: Feverfew does well in a large pot in a sunny situation.

Size: Grows to a height of 30-60 cm.

Harvesting: Leaves and flowers can be picked at any time. If the flowering head is allowed to set seed the plant will not remain perennial, so cut the flowers and enjoy them in vases.

Dos and don'ts: Feverfew makes an excellent companion plant for vegetables like lettuce, spinach, radish, peas, beans and squashes. The leaves make an excellent insect repellent if mixed into a spray.

USES
Domestic
☐ An infusion of the leaf serves as a mild disinfectant.
☐ Dried feverfew leaves in sachets deter moths.
☐ When added to tansy leaves and flowers, feverfew can be made into an insect-repellent posy, and the dried flowers in potpourris add colour and serve to keep insects away.
☐ A few chopped feverfew leaves added to washing up water will cut the grease on the dishes. Alternatively, soak the leaves in a greasy pot with hot water. After an hour or two you will be able to wash it out easily.

Cosmetic
☐ Feverfew leaves were used as early as the 17th century in the first commercial skin lotion, which was said to remove freckles and blemishes, but due to its bitter smell it has now been replaced by other herbs for this purpose.

Medicinal
☐ Feverfew was used hundreds, if not thousands, of years ago as a general tonic. As its name suggests, it was thought of as a substance that reduces fever. It is also associated with "women's" ailments, and was once used to help in labour and to promote menstruation, as well as a suppository for painful piles.
☐ Migraine sufferers may find relief by eating 1^1/$_2$ big leaves or 3 small leaves daily in sandwiches for a period up to a year. Rheumatism sufferers have also reported good results.
☐ An infusion may be used as a mouthwash after tooth extraction, and it is also a mild laxative. In the olden days it was used to cure fever, melancholy and vertigo.
☐ The leaf may be infused to produce a mild sedative and appetite stimulant, and also to relieve muscle spasms. Steep a small leaf in a cup of boiling water and allow to stand for just five minutes. Strain and sip a small quantity with lemon juice.

Culinary
☐ The leaf has a very bitter flavour, but reduces greasiness when added in tiny amounts to fatty food like ham, pork sausages or suet puddings.
☐ NOTE: Feverfew and chamomile are often confused as they have similar flowers.

GARLIC/KNOFFEL
Allium sativum
Family: Liliaceae

Garlic is a member of the onion family and is universally used as a flavouring in cooking. It has been cultivated for centuries and never seems to have lost its popularity. The ancient Egyptians and Romans used it medicinally; the slaves who constructed the pyramid of Cheops were fed garlic daily to sustain their strength. There are several varieties of garlic, varying in flavour and strength.

CULTIVATION

Garlic is an annual. It is an undemanding plant to grow and only takes up a little space.

Conditions: Garlic needs full sun, and prefers a light, well-drained soil.

Propagation: In spring by seeds, bulblets or cloves. Plant individual cloves broken off from the main bulb in well-dug soil to which a spadeful or two of well-rotted manure has been added and thoroughly dug into the soil. Space the cloves 15 cm apart and 5 cm deep. Keep moist until they shoot, thereafter water well every few days. They will benefit from a leaf mulch to keep the soil cool, moist and friable. Leave to mature for the full season, and reap before the frost.

Seed can be sown in seed trays filled with sand in spring or autumn. Keep moist and protected until well up, then harden off by placing in the sun for longer periods of time each day. Do not allow to dry out. Plant 15 cm apart when big enough to handle.

Size: Grows to a height of 30 cm.

Harvesting: Dried garlic cloves maintain their medicinal properties for months, so it's easy to have some at hand all the time. Allow the bulbs to mature and top growth to dry and die down before reaping. Stop watering when the leaves start to turn yellow and pull up before the flower appears.

Dos and don'ts: Garlic grown near roses deters greenfly. Garlic will inhibit the growth of peas and beans.

USES

Domestic

☐ Put some chopped garlic in your dog's food to keep him free from ticks and fleas.

☐ Peeled and finely chopped cloves of garlic are an essential standby for curing coccycidiosis in poultry.

☐ Cloves of garlic, slightly crushed, can be placed in food containers, wheat and mealie bins, to keep them free of weevils.

☐ A garlic extract can be used to control aphids. Add two crushed cloves of garlic to 570 ml of water and spray on afflicted plants. Add strongly scented plants like rue or basil for best effect.

☐ Garlic can also be used to keep ants away. Pound 4 garlic bulbs. To 4 litres of boiling water add 250 ml washing powder, 4 handfuls of khakibos leaves and the crushed garlic. Mix and pour into antholes.

☐ A spray for potato and tomato blight can be made from chopped garlic and onions. Chop 2 bulbs of garlic and 4 large onions, boil with 3 litres of water, cool and strain. Use shortly after preparing.

Medicinal

☐ Fresh garlic included daily in the diet is beneficial for so many different disorders that it is difficult to list them all. It is used in medicine as an antibacterial and expectorant, and to treat hypertension, arteriosclerosis, dysentery, the common cold (see recipe below), typhoid and bronchial catarrh.

☐ It is useful as an antiseptic, general tonic and worm deterrent and is considered to have antibiotic properties.

☐ Garlic is used to treat fevers and blood disorders, tuberculosis, whooping cough, asthma, obesity, rheumatism and arthritis. Consumption of garlic can help the body resist many infectious diseases.

☐ The Xhosa people drink a decoction of the leaf and bulb as a febrifuge (to reduce fever), sometimes adding wild wormwood (*Artemisia afra*).

☐ An old folk remedy for rheumatism is made by mashing garlic with honey; rub it onto the afflicted areas.

☐ A poultice of the garlic bulb applied to the temples has long been used as a headache remedy and also to relieve insect, scorpion and centipede bites.

☐ In India garlic is rubbed over window sills and around doorways to repel snakes, and the warmed juice is used in drop form for earache.

☐ Diluted garlic juice can be used to wash wounds.

☐ Inhalations of garlic fumes (created by pouring boiling water over chopped garlic and producing steam, which is inhaled) have traditionally been used to treat all lung ailments, including tuberculosis, bronchitis and pneumonia.

☐ In most treatments it is preferable to eat the garlic raw, chopping the leaves and cloves and adding to salads or eating on bread, but chopped garlic cloves can be added to bread dough before baking or to vegetables while cooking. Plenty of fresh parsley may be chewed to cleanse the odour from the breath.

☐ Colds and fevers may be treated by eating a raw clove three times a day, or by drinking the juice. The following chest cold and asthma syrup is also effective. Peel and chop three garlic cloves and simmer in 625 ml water until the liquid is reduced by half. Remove the garlic by straining through a sieve and then add 185 ml apple cider vinegar and 100 g of sugar or honey. Place the garlic in a bottle and then cover with the syrup. One dessertspoonful should be taken each night. Store in fridge

☐ Make a corn cure by placing a fresh piece of garlic on a bandage and binding it in position over the corn. Replace with fresh garlic each day and repeat for ten days.

Culinary

☐ Garlic is a very strong flavouring and can be used in most savoury dishes, whether hot or cold.

☐ Garlic is delicious in salad dressings and marinades.

☐ It can be used to make garlic vinegar and oil.

☐ Chopped garlic can be added to butter to make garlic butter, and is an essential ingredient in many dips.

☐ The bulb can be baked whole and eaten as a vegetable.

☐ Garlic leaves have a more subtle flavour than bulbs, and can be used chopped finely in dishes that require a more delicate taste.

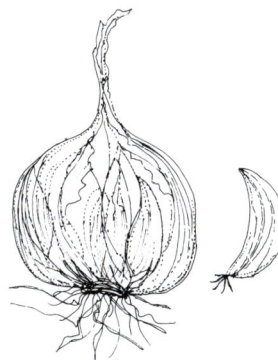

Garlic butter

1 cup soft butter
4–8 cloves garlic, peeled and finely chopped
 (or 1 teaspoon garlic flakes)
about ¼ teaspoon salt

Choose a fresh French loaf or bake a loaf of wholewheat bread. Slice fairly thickly, but do not slice right through. Butter each slice on both sides with the well-blended garlic butter. Wrap in aluminium foil and place in a hot oven for 10 – 15 minutes or until the bread is crisp and golden. Serve hot.

Garlic vinegar

This can be used on its own as a salad dressing, combined with oils and mustard into a delicious dressing, or used whenever a dish calls for a flavoured vinegar. It is strong and wonderfully versatile, and can be stored for many months. Whenever I have a crop of matured garlic I immediately make enough vinegar to last me for a season. Remember you will have to make enough to give away, as this is a cook's favourite.

1 bottle white vinegar
2 garlic bulbs, broken into cloves

Push the garlic cloves into the bottle of white vinegar, bruising and peeling each clove before popping it into the bottle. Stand the bottle in the sun for 100 hours of strong sunlight – I leave it for about 2 weeks in a good sunny position. Taste, and if it is not strong enough, repeat the procedure. Strain through muslin into a clean, attractive bottle, push in a few thinly peeled fresh cloves and, if you can, a garlic flower and a few leaves. This makes the bottle attractive and easy to identify on the kitchen shelf.

HONEYSUCKLE/KANFERFOELIE (KAMFERFOELIE)

Lonicera periclymenum
Family: Caprifoliaceae

This creeper is a well loved garden plant all over the world. Not only is it beautiful, it has a lovely fragrance and a multitude of medicinal uses. The whole plant is medicinal, said to be good for rheumatism, arthritis and the treatment of wounds, among other things. Honeysuckle is also known as "woodbine" overseas. There are many Lonicera varieties, all exquisite in potpourris.

CULTIVATION

Honeysuckle is a perennial climber that needs very little attention apart from the occasional watering and trimming. Where tendrils touch the ground they send down roots and these can be cut away and replanted.

Conditions: Honeysuckle likes sun or partial shade and an average soil.

Propagation: By cutting or rooted runners. In the case of runners, cut away and replant then keep moist for a few days until established.

Size: Grows up to 3 m tall and covers trellises, fences and pergolas with a neat, evergreen abundance.

Harvesting: Pick flowers any time of year – midsummer is best.

Dos and don'ts: Honeysuckle can be used to cover banks, fences, arbours and shade houses if tied to supports and the unruly tendrils trimmed. Honeysuckle will attract butterflies to your garden and is one of the most popular fragrant climbers.

USES

Domestic

☐ Honeysuckle is ideal as a cut flower (yellow and pink) for vases, with the added benefit of a sweet smell.

☐ The fragrant honeysuckle flowers are a wonderful addition to potpourri and can be used in pillow sachets.

Medicinal

☐ Honeysuckle flowers can be used to make an asthma treatment. Combine with equal parts of honey and molasses and take a teaspoonful morning and night.

☐ A tea can be made by adding a quarter cup of flowers to a cup of boiling water. Let stand for five minutes and sip in the morning on rising to soothe sore throats, ease joint stiffness and relieve arthritis or rheumatism.

☐ The flowers can be preserved in honey for use in medicinal remedies for winter ailments like coughs, colds, sore throats, flu, fever and chills. Take a teaspoonful at a time. Pack a jar with the flowers and pour just enough honey in the jar to cover them. Store in a cool cupboard.

☐ Crushed leaves, warmed in hot water, can be applied to wounds and sores to help heal them.

☐ Make a brew from a cup of crushed honeysuckle leaves to one litre of boiling water. Stand for 15 minutes then strain. Apply to rashes – it will clear them up if used daily.

LEMON BALM/SUURLEMOEN KRUISEMENT
Melissa officinalis
Family: Labiatae

This attractive garden plant, a member of the mint family, is rewarding to grow as it has a lot of medicinal and culinary uses. The herb is popular all over the world, and is commonly known as melissa. The leaves are used to make a fragrant oil used in the perfume industry. The plant is also known as lemon mint. It is the sweetest of all herbs. It is indigenous to the mountainous regions of southern Europe and was introduced into Britain by the Romans. It was sacred to the temple of Diana and used by the ancient Greeks for medical purposes some 2 000 years ago. The Swiss physician Paracelsus called it the "elixir of life." It has always been associated with the relieving of melancholy, and is used today in aromatherapy to combat depression.

CULTIVATION
Melissa is a hardy perennial that is easy to grow.
Conditions: Likes moist, rich soils and filtered shade. It dies down in winter and benefits from being cut back hard to encourage its new spring growth.
Propagation: By cuttings or division. Take cuttings of new growth in midsummer and press into sand. Keep them uniformly moist for a week or two, and they will root in no time. Plant out 30 cm apart and keep damp for the first two or three weeks; thereafter water twice a week. At the end of summer cut straggly growth, lift and separate encroaching plants into new areas.
Containers: Small plants can be grown indoors as pot plants. They need a little light and sun.

Size: Up to 50 cm.
Harvesting: The leaves can be picked any time, but must be handled carefully to prevent bruising.
Dos and don'ts: Do plant melissa if you want to attract bees to your garden. Melissa has a generally beneficial effect on surrounding plants. It does well tucked behind and between taller growers. It loves being picked.

USES
Domestic
☐ Melissa leaves are an ingredient in potpourris, and if hung in bunches in cupboards they deter moths.
☐ A mixture of melissa and marjoram (a cup of each boiled in 2 *l* of water for 10 min, then cooked and strained) is given to cows to help them recover after calving.
☐ In beekeeping, when a new swarm comes to a hive rub the inside of the hive with a handful of melissa leaves and the bees will never leave it.
☐ Melissa is excellent for polishing wooden furniture if a handful of green leaves are rubbed over the wooden surface. The oil in the leaves is absorbed by the wood and the crushed leaves impart a lingering lemony fragrance. It refreshes a smoke-filled atmosphere.

Cosmetic
☐ Use the leaf in infusions for facials, and as a rinse for greasy hair.
☐ Add melissa leaves to bath water and to vinegar for rinsing the hair. Mixed with aqueous cream they have a soothing effect when rubbed into aching feet.

Medicinal
☐ Hot melissa tea has a reviving effect and helps settle nerves; it is also beneficial for coughs and colds and effective in combating insomnia, depression, indigestion, anxiety, tension, stress, fear and panic. Make it by adding one or two thumb-length sprigs to a cup of boiling water. Allow it to stand for 5 minutes then strain and sweeten with a little honey if liked.
☐ Cool lemon balm tea will soothe anyone who has been bitten by insects or by a dog, or is upset or anxious.
☐ The leaves can be placed fresh directly onto insect bites and sores, or applied as a poultice.

Culinary
☐ Melissa leaves can be used in fruit salads and to make a cooling summer drink. Pour a litre of boiling water over a cup of leaves, cool, strain and add the juice of 2 lemons and a litre of clear apple juice. Add honey to sweeten if necessary and serve chilled.
Served warm, this drink is excellent in combating indigestion and can be drunk after a heavy meal as it will help to digest fatty dishes.
☐ Freeze a sprig of lemon balm in ice cubes to decorate and flavour drinks.
☐ Because of its lemony flavour melissa is delicious with fish and cheese dishes. It combines well with cucumber, celery and asparagus.

LAVENDER/LAVENTEL
Lavandula species
Family: Labiatae   *English lavender (L. angustifolia)*

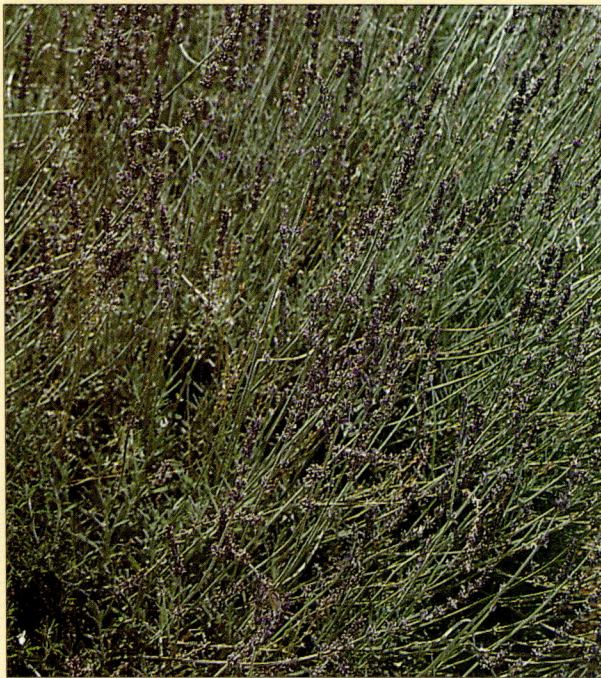

The beautifully fragrant lavender plant is an asset to any herb garden and is probably the most popular herb of all. It has long been used to freshen the air in houses, and the Romans and Greeks added it to their bath water. In fact its name derives from the Latin word "lavare," meaning "to wash." Besides its prized aromatic qualities it is also used for culinary and medicinal purposes. It has been used for its sedative and antiseptic properties, as well as its insect repelling qualities, for many centuries. The most widely used varieties are English lavender, Lavandula angustifolia, and L. spica, which both become rather tall. Two dwarf varieties, L. vera (Dutch lavender) and L. spica (Munstead) are available in South Africa. They grow to about 30 cm in height. French lavender, Lavandula dentata, is a showy plant that reaches about 90 cm in height, and is particularly attractive and aromatic, with short bud-like flowers, but has no medicinal use. Spike lavender or L. latifolia is particularly fragrant.

CULTIVATION
Lavender is a perennial plant.
Conditions: Lavender likes dry, well-drained soil and a sunny position.
Propagation: Can be done from seeds or cuttings. Cuttings can be pulled from the stems at any time of the year except the coldest months. Make sure that a "heel" is torn off with the cutting and press securely into wet sand. In April and May make a polythene tent to put over the cutting tray to keep it protected and moist. In June, July and August all cuttings benefit from a plastic tent as it acts as a miniature hothouse. The newly rooted plants should be well protected against the cold. The seed germinates easily if sown in river sand and kept damp. Plant seedlings 90 cm apart; 45 cm in the case of the dwarf species.
Size: Varies from 30 to 120 cm depending on species.
Harvesting: Cut bushes back to encourage bushy compact growth and dry the twigs you remove. They can be dried by hanging in bunches or laying out on trays. Flowering stems can be gathered just as the flower opens, and leaves can be picked at any time.
Dos and don'ts: Lavender can be badly affected by frost in winter, and it is a good idea to cover the bushes with grass if you live in a frost-susceptible area. Lavender has the habit of suddenly dying off for no apparent reason. If the whole bush dies, it is best to remove it completely and replace the soil around the root area with fresh soil. Dig in a little compost and plant a new bush in its place. Always have a few cuttings or seedlings on standby in case your bushes do die suddenly. Lavender will encourage butterflies to visit your garden. It will repel moths, however. Grow lavender near scented geraniums, as each enhances the other's perfume. Lavender also grows well near or interspersed with legumes. Lavender makes an ideal hedging plant and withstands constant clipping.

USES
Domestic
☐ Lavender is an essential ingredient in potpourri.
☐ Lavender sachets can be hung in linen cupboards to keep linen fresh. Add 10 parts lavender leaves and flowers to 2 parts minced, dried lemon peel, and one part each of coriander seeds, cinnamon pieces and cloves. Mix well, add lavender essential oil, and seal in a crock or jar. Shake daily for two weeks, adding more oil if desired, then fill sachets or pillows.
☐ Dried stalks of lavender can be placed on fires in winter; they produce a lovely scent which pervades the whole house.
☐ Keep away fish moths by hanging bags filled with lavender and crushed cloves, with a little lavender oil added. Mice also hate the smell of lavender
☐ If you spread your washing over lavender bushes to dry it will remain sweet-smelling and fresh for a long time.

Cosmetic
☐ Lavender flowers can be used to make a tonic water for delicate and sensitive skins, and it has an antiseptic effect beneficial to acne suffers.

Medicinal

☐ A lavender-stuffed pillow aids sleep and will soothe and calm a restless child.

☐ Lavender tea can be drunk to relieve headaches and exhaustion, promote sleep and relieve anxiety. Make it by pouring 250 ml of boiling water over a thumb-length sprig of leaves, stand for five minutes, then strain and sweeten with honey. A few drops of lavender water on a handkerchief held over the brow will also relieve headaches. Or make your own lavender headache cure by boiling 440 ml lavender flowers in water, then cool and strain. Place the flowers in a screw-top jar, then cover with 310 ml apple cider vinegar. Leave for a week in a cool, dark place. Shake well daily, and after a week strain the liquid through muslin and discard the lavender flowers. Add 310 ml cooled rosewater and bottle. Saturate a wad of cotton wool with the potion to relieve headaches and place on temples or forehead. Splash on tired feet and wrists to combat fatigue.

☐ Lavender water makes an excellent mouthwash.

Culinary

☐ Lavender flowers can be sprinkled over a fruit salad. Choose fresh young flowers and break them up finely before sprinkling. Added to white grape vinegar, lavender flowers are excellent in soothing aching legs. Add the mixture to the bath or rub into tired feet. Add a small bunch of lavender to the bath for a relaxing soak after a tiring day.

☐ Lavender is an excellent addition to marinades for game. It also has the effect of tenderising tough meat. Wrap the meat in the leaves and keep overnight in the fridge.

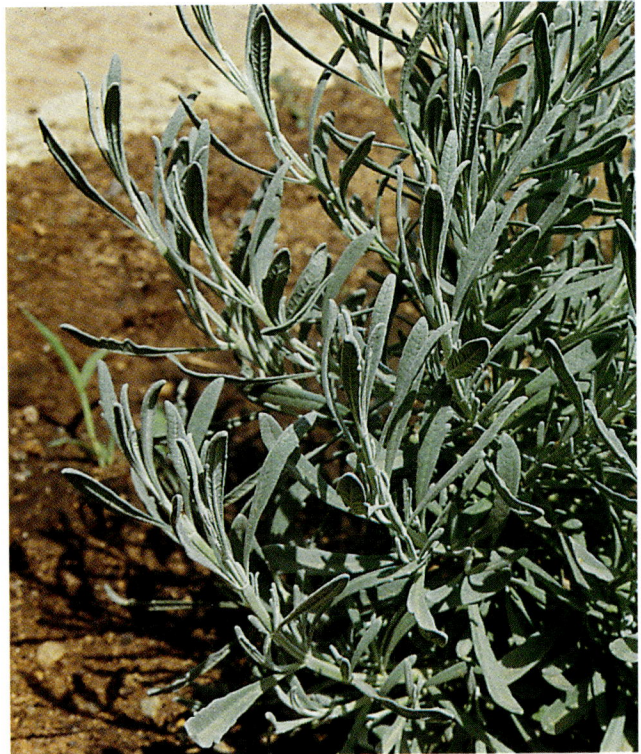

Lavender spica

☐ Lavender leaves can be added to stews and braised meat dishes. Use about 1 tablespoon of fresh chopped leaves per dish.

☐ Lavender sugar, made by mixing 750 g white sugar with 4 cups of lavender flowers (on the stalks) and mixing them in a blender, can be used for baking and confectionery to add a subtle flavour.

Lavender honey

This is an excellent cough remedy and soothing agent for sore throats, and gives a delicious flavouring to herb teas and fruit drinks.

1 cupful lavender leaves
500 g honey

Place the lavender leaves in a pot. Pour the honey over them. Heat gently over a pot of boiling water (a double boiler is perfect), cover and simmer for half an hour. Pour into hot jars and seal. Store for at least one month before using. Strain through a sieve, discard the flowers and store in screw-top honey jars.

Lavender tea

This refreshing tea is quick and easy to make and will alleviate fatigue and stress.

2 fresh lavender sprays, or 2 – 4 teaspoons flowers stripped of their stems, or a thumb-length leafy twig
1 cup boiling water

Pour the boiling water over the lavender. Stand a few minutes, sweeten with lavender honey if desired, and sip while inhaling the aroma. Herb tea should never be drunk with milk and the only sweetening should be honey.

Rose petal, orange blossom, honeysuckle and jasmine honey can also be made in this way. Orange blossom is bitter so do not leave it too long.

LEMON GRASS/SITROENGRAS
Cymbopogan citratus
Family: Gramineae

Lemon grass was once rare and seldom used, but like many other formerly obscure herbs it is increasing rapidly in popularity. It is indigenous to the tropics and grows to a height of 1,8 m. It has fragrant, very long, thin leaves and greenish/red flowers that appear in clusters.

As its name suggests, lemon grass has a lemony flavour and aroma, and is useful both as a culinary and medicinal herb.

CULTIVATION
Lemon grass can be grown in any soil and needs very little water. It is sensitive to frost and dormant in winter.

Propagation: Clumps can be divided and side roots and shoots separated and replanted.

Size: It grows to a height of 1,8 m.

Dos and don'ts: Do cut regularly for a luxuriant growth.

USES
Domestic
☐ To spread a lemony fragrance through your house add lemon grass to warmed furniture polish or to warmed aqueous cream which is then added to furniture polish. This is excellent for clearing a smoky room.

☐ To rid your house of the smell of smoke, add lemon grass to a lemon potpourri. Combine with equal quantities of lemon verbena, lemon thyme and lemon balm, and add one cup of dried lemon peel and half a cup of cloves for every six cups of leaves. Add lemon or lemon verbena essential oil, keep sealed for a week, shaking daily, before filling bowls and sachets.

Cosmetic
☐ An infusion of lemon grass – one cup of fresh lemon grass to two cups of boiling water – makes an excellent wash for oily skins.

☐ Use the same brew to rinse oily hair. Dilute with two or more cups of warm water for a scalp treatment to prevent dandruff. The same mixture can be combed into unmanageable hair as a setting lotion.

☐ It makes a good astringent facial steam for teenage skins.

Medicinal
☐ Lemon grass tea has a calming effect as well as soothing the digestion and alleviating stress. Use it as a substitute for ordinary tea. It's delicious both hot and cold.

Culinary
☐ Lemon grass is best known as a fragrant flavouring in teas and drinks.

☐ A few blades of lemon grass added to any dish gives a delicious lemon flavour. Try adding a small bundle to soups and stews while they are cooking. It can be combined with other herbs, but only with the more subtle ones as its delicate flavour is easily overpowered.

☐ The tender stalks can be chopped finely into salads.

☐ A leaf of lemon grass added to rice or pasta enhances the dish.

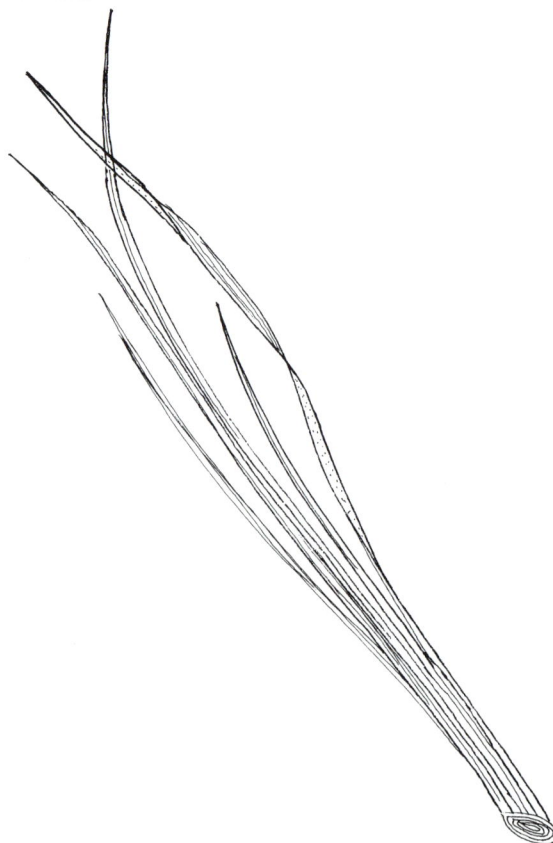

LEMON VERBENA/YSTERKRUID
Aloysia triphylla (*Lippia citriodora*)
Family: Verbenaceae

This plant is most prized for the lovely sharp lemony fragrance of its leaves; it is one of the most aromatic of all shrubs. Indigenous to South America, it was brought to Europe by the Spanish in the seventeenth century and cultivated for its oil. It was also added to finger bowl water. Not only is lemon verbena invaluable for its aromatic leaves with their multitude of uses, it is also a very pretty shrub in garden.

CULTIVATION
Lemon verbena is a semi-hardy shrub that is grown indoors and in greenhouses in Europe. On the South African Highveld it loses its leaves in winter and should be covered with grass or hessian in the frost.

Conditions:
Lemon verbena requires full sun, and a sheltered and frost-free position. The soil it is grown in should be light, well-drained and alkaline. The poorer the soil, the stronger the plants.

Propagation: Take cuttings in summer. Choose woody pieces with a small heel, trim off the excess leaves and press into wet sand. Keep them cool, shaded, moist and protected and plant into bags when rooted to establish a sturdy plant. Plant them 1 m apart, as the plant grows as wide as it does tall. Prune the branches to encourage new growth.

Size: The plant reaches a height of between 1,5 and 2 m and grows into a bushy shrub.

Harvesting: Leaves can be picked any time. Cut off the flowering tips if you want the plant to become thick and bushy, and trim it regularly.

Dos and don'ts: Do plant lemon verbena if you want to attract butterflies to your garden. The plants benefit from a good spray of water every now and then. Heavy wind can break the branches of the plant so stake them if they are too heavy or long. It benefits from pruning.

USES
Domestic
☐ The dried leaves retain their scent for a very long time and can be used in potpourri.
☐ Twigs and even fresh leaves can be put into cupboards to keep linen fresh and scented.

Cosmetic
☐ Lemon verbena leaves can be macerated in almond oil to produce an aromatic oil for massage. It can be blended with other fragrant oils if desired, and added to home-made cosmetics.
☐ An infusion of lemon verbena applied to the eyes with cotton wool and left for 15 minutes relieves puffiness. Pour 1 cup boiling water over 1 tablespoon of crushed leaves and steep for 10 minutes, then strain and cool.
☐ Lemon verbena leaves (tied into a facecloth or placed in a sachet) can be added to a bath for aromatic effect.

Medicinal
☐ The leaf can be infused to make a mildly sedative tea that soothes bronchial and nasal congestion, indigestion, flatulence, stomach cramps and nausea. The tea is made by adding 4-8 leaves to 1 cup of boiling water, sweetened with honey if desired. It should be drunk after meals.

Culinary
☐ Lemon verbena leaf can be used to make a herb tea that is particularly refreshing if drunk after eating rich food (see recipe above). The leaves can also be made into an excellent base for cool drinks. Pour 1 *l* of boiling water over a cup of lemon verbena leaves and allow to cool. Add 1,5 *l* fruit juice, sweeten with honey and chill.
☐ The leaf can be finely chopped and used in hot drinks, puddings, jellies, cakes, etc.
☐ Lemon verbena leaves, chopped and sprinkled with fresh lemon juice, do wonders for the flavour of grilled fish.
☐ Cook rice with a sprig of lemon verbena to give it a delicate flavour. Remove the sprig before serving.
☐ Add a sprig to oatmeal porridge for an unusual flavour.

LOVAGE/LAVAS
Levisticum officinale
Family: Umbelliferae

This very attractive plant has a strong flavour and is an interesting culinary herb. It was once used to make a reviving cordial served at wayside inns. Lovage seed can still be used to make a reviving drink by adding it to brandy and sweetening with sugar. The leaf is used in cooking. Lovage is a close relative of celery, but is four times the size.

CULTIVATION
Lovage is a hardy herbaceous perennial with distinctive greenish yellow lacy flowers borne in clusters.

Conditions: Lovage thrives in partial shade, and likes a rich, moist, cool soil that should be well composted twice yearly. It dies down in winter.

Propagation: Seeds can be sown in trays in March, for planting out in September. Seed is not easily available in South Africa, so look out for seedlings at your local nursery. Thin or transplant seedlings to 60 cm apart. The plants don't seem to mind being moved when young, as long as enough soil is removed with the roots. Root cuttings can be taken in spring or autumn.

Size: Grows to between 1 and 1,2 m in height including flowering head.

Harvesting: Leaves can be picked any time, but the young central leaves should be left on the plant. Seed can be gathered when ripe. When the plant dies down in winter pick and dry several bunches of leaves to use in soups and stews. Dry on a newspaper in the shade, turning every day, then when dry store in well-stoppered glass bottles in a dark cupboard.

Dos and don'ts: Lovage does not do well near fennel, and needs to have the soil loosened around it to encourage its growth. Cover with compost or mulch well in winter to protect the "crown."

USES
Cosmetic
☐ Lovage makes an excellent deodorant, used as a wash or a gargle. Make it by pouring a litre of boiling water over a cup of leaves, then cool and strain.

Medicinal
☐ The seed, leaf or root can be infused to make a tea to reduce water retention and act as a purifier. It is also said to help against rheumatism, but should not be drunk during pregnancy or by those with kidney problems. The recipe is 2 teaspoonfuls of seeds or chopped roots, or a quarter cup of fresh leaves. Pour a cup of boiling water over this, stand for five minutes and strain.

☐ Lovage is noted for its efficacy in relieving coughs and treating stomach disorders. Add it to soups and salads and drink a little in the form of a tea. The Romans added the seeds and finely chopped leaves to salads to ease stomach pains brought on by overeating.

Culinary
☐ Lovage can be dried and used in mixed herb sachets or bouquet garni bags – but it has a strong flavour and should be used sparingly.

☐ Lovage seed is added to liqueurs and cordials to provide flavour. It can also be crushed in breads and pastries, and sprinkled in small quantities on salads and mashed potatoes.

☐ Lovage leaves give soups, stock and stews a delicious flavour. It is often called the "Maggi" herb, because of its meaty flavour so typical of "Maggi" brand sauces. The leaf can also be rubbed on chicken before cooking to impart flavour.

☐ The root can be cooked (whole or grated) or pickled.

☐ The stems may be cooked on their own as a vegetable or chopped and added to peas and served with butter and lemon juice.

MARJORAM/MARJOLEIN
Origanum majorana
Family: Labiatae

Marjoram is particularly valued for its sweet, spicy scent, which is said to have been created by Aphrodite as a symbol of happiness. Marjoram plants were once placed on tombs to ensure peace for departed spirits, and it was said to be an antidote to poisoning. A native of the Mediterranean, it was in great demand in the middle ages for posies and pot-pourris. It is related to oregano, O. vulgare.
O. majorana is also known as sweet or knotted mar-joram.

CULTIVATION
Sweet marjoram is a semi-hardy perennial with white flowers and pale green leaves.

Conditions: Likes full sun but happily takes a bit of shade in the afternoons and although not fussy about soil type, prefers a sandy soil. It should not be grown in the heavier clay type soil, unless lots of friable material has been dug in.

Propagation: By cuttings. Where branches touch the ground they will often send out rootlets, and these can be cut away and planted elsewhere. Take cuttings from the previous year's growth in midsummer or spring, and keep in moist sand until rooted. Plant out where desired but keep in shade for a few days. Cut back flowering stems to retain bush shape. You'll be able to cut back and prune the plants three times a year.

Containers: Marjoram makes a good container plant if planted in a large, deep pot with good drainage, but it does need full sun.

Size: Grows to 30 to 60 cm in height.

Harvesting: Harvest when the flowers start maturing into seeds. All parts can be used, and young leafy sprigs can be picked all year round.

Dos and don'ts: Marjoram will benefit almost any plant it is grown in proximity with. Do grow marjoram if you want to attract bees and butterflies to your garden, and use it to edge beds near roses – it helps repel aphids.

USES
Domestic
☐ Sweet marjoram leaves were used to polish furniture and floors in the past, and the pulverised leaves can be added to furniture polish to give a fresh, fragrant aroma.
☐ Use sweet marjoram leaves in potpourri and air fresheners.

Cosmetic
☐ Chew a sprig to get rid of bad breath.

Medicinal
☐ Chew a sprig of marjoram to relieve sore throats and ease coughing.
☐ The flowering top of sweet marjoram can be infused to make a tea to treat colds, headaches, nervous and stomach disorders. To make the standard brew pour a cup of boiling water over a quarter cup leaves, flowers and sprigs. Stand for 5 minutes and strain; add a little honey if desired.
☐ The essential oil or decoction of marjoram leaves in oil can be added to ointments, bathwater or compresses to relieve rheumatic pains and tension. A few drops sprinkled on a pillow will promote sleep.

Culinary
☐ The leaf of sweet marjoram may be infused to make an aromatic tea (see standard brew, above).
☐ Chop leaves finely to add to salads and butter sauces.
☐ Chopped leaves can be added to meat dishes when nearly cooked.
☐ Marjoram can be used in fish and chicken dishes.
☐ Lay marjoram stems on a braai grid to give the food a subtle flavour.
☐ Marjoram dries well, and in this form makes a delicious addition to scrambled eggs.
☐ Use dried marjoram seed heads in savoury herb mixes and bouquet garnis. Dry them out on newspaper in the shade for two or three days, then rub off the stem and store in crocks or bottles. Keep airtight. For a "pinch of herbs" mix 1 part each of dried thyme, celery leaves, and marjoram with half a part of crushed coriander seed.

MINT/KRUISEMENT
Mentha species
Family: Labiatae

Pineapple mint
(M. sauveolens "variegata")

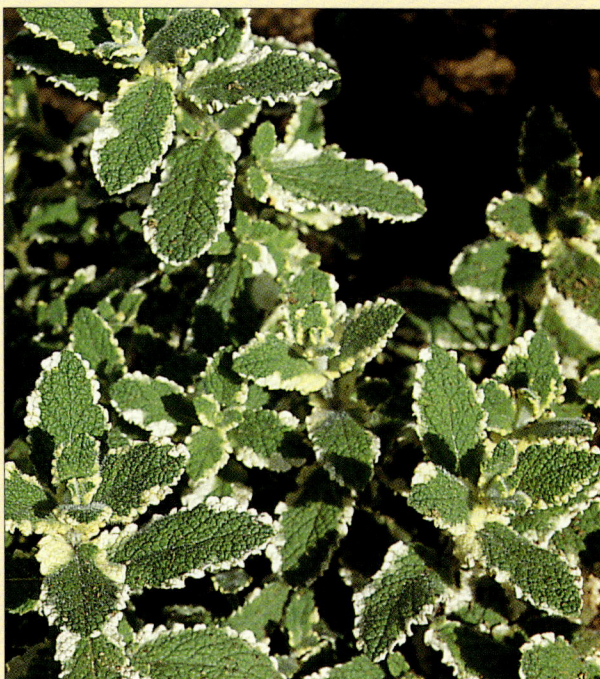

The mint family has more than 600 members and has been esteemed all over the world for thousands of years for its versatility. Mint, traditionally regarded as a symbol of hospitality, is said to have been named after Minthe, a nymph in Greek mythology. Pluto, the god of the underworld, fell in love with her, and his wife Proserpine became so jealous that she transformed her into this scented herb. In Biblical times the Pharisees paid tax with mint leaves. The most distinguishing feature of mint is its fresh, pungent taste and fragrance. It is a very useful culinary and medicinal herb.

Mint is often difficult to classify because the various species interbreed readily. Two of the most popular varieties are M. aquatica (spearmint or wild water mint), which grows wild in certain well-watered parts of South Africa, and M. spicata (garden mint). M. citrata (orange mint), peppermint (M. piperita), pennyroyal (M. pulegium), jewel mint (M. requienii), apple mint (M. sauveolens), pineapple or golden apple mint (M. sauveolens "variegata"), chocolate mint and a pretty, tall-growing tuft with dark hairy leaves called "Cape velvet mint" are some other members of the species.

CULTIVATION
Mint is a hardy herbaceous perennial.

Conditions: The mints like a rich, moist, well-drained alkaline soil, but they will grow anywhere moist!

Propagation: By root or stem cuttings, or divide the plant. The mints readily invade neighbouring beds, but can be contained by placing thick strips of black plastic vertically in furrows around the mint beds. After three years all mints should be lifted and replanted in newly composted soil. The plants are always seeking new ground and so constantly send out runners, often dying off untidily from behind; old roots should be discarded and new runners reset in fresh soil.

Pineapple mint is particularly easy to grow, and is used as a ground cover as it does not need as much water as other varieties. It grows to 30 cm and forms an attractive bush if clipped back and trimmed. Apple mint also withstands drought and full sun. It grows to about 40 cm and has a furry, greyish-green leaf. Orange mint and eau de cologne mint like shade and a moist soil but can be grown in the sun. Both grow to about 30 cm and are worth cultivating for their pleasant fragrance. Jewel mint is a very small variety, seldom growing to more than 3 cm in height. It requires a lot of water and prefers shade. It has a wonderful fragrance. *M. spicata*, the common or garden variety, tends to grow under the dripping garden tap and reaches a height of 30-50 cm. *M. aquatica*, as its name suggests, likes wet feet but can be grown in a sunny situation. This variety is also commonly called spearmint and can grow up to 1 m in height in tall flower-topped sprays – it has long pointed leaves.

Containers: Mint can be grown in containers. It should be repotted every year, preferably in early spring, and watered daily. Give it an occasional dressing of organic plant food like marinure. It needs a bit of sun daily, so don't keep the pot in full shade.

Size: 3 cm – 1 m, depending on species.

Harvesting: Pick leaves at any time of year – the best time is just before the plant flowers.

Dos and don'ts: Do keep different types of mint apart, as they are very invasive and interbreed easily. You can help prevent this by keeping the flowering heads cut so that the bees cannot cross-pollinate. More vigorous types may also swamp the slower-growing varieties. Do grow pennyroyal near roses to keep aphids away. Mints do not like manure, so prepare beds for mint with compost and leaf mould only. The more you cut it the better it grows, but constantly replace old mother roots with new runners and add lots of compost.

USES
Domestic
☐ Hang bunches of fresh mint in your kitchen to keep flies away. Bruise the bunches from time to time, and replace them when they dry out. Rub peppermint into the skin to repel mosquitoes. Test a little on the inside of the wrist first.

☐ Scatter fresh or dried leaves around food to keep mice away.

□ Pennyroyal can be placed in cupboards and beds to keep away ants and fleas, and rubbed on blankets, pillows and clothing to keep mosquitoes away. A tub of pennyroyal on the patio is an excellent fly and mosquito deterrent.

□ The dried leaf is an aromatic addition to potpourri and sachets.

Cosmetic

□ Spearmint can be used to make a decoction for chapped hands, and added to the bathwater for an invigorating soak.

□ A fresh handful of jewel mint, peppermint, spearmint or eau de cologne mint placed in a muslin bag can also be added to bathwater to ease tiredness and general aches and pains.

Medicinal

□ In ancient times mint was used to cure all manner of conditions, including the bite of mad dogs and vipers, stings, mouth and gum infections and digestive troubles, not to mention skin disorders. It is important to note that *pennyroyal* should not be taken by pregnant women or anyone suffering from kidney problems. Rather use the other mints instead.

□ Chewing a mint leaf aids in digestion.

□ An infusion of mint may be inhaled to relieve colds and congestion. Pour a litre of boiling water over a bowl of mint (about a cup and a half of fresh sprigs), cover the head and the bowl with a towel and inhale the steam.

□ Peppermint can be infused to make a tea which relieves cold and influenza symptoms and digestive trouble. Sip cold for flatulence and hiccups. Make it by pouring a cup of boiling water over a quarter cup of fresh leaves; stand for five minutes and then strain.

□ Spearmint and peppermint leaves can be macerated in almond oil then massaged into the temples to relieve migraines and muscular pains.

Culinary

□ Mint leaves can be infused to make a delicious and refreshing tea. Make as above. Do not use jewel mint or pennyroyal for this purpose, though, as they are too strong and bitter-tasting. If you have more than one type of mint try blending them to obtain a more interesting flavour.

□ Garden mint is the favourite variety for mint sauce, an indispensable condiment for lamb. Chop half a cup of mint leaves finely, add half a cup each of sugar, vinegar and warm water. Mix well.

□ Mint is delicious in sweet sauces, jellies and fruit drinks. It is an excellent garnish for fruit salads.

□ Mint can be crystallised as a decoration for sweet dishes and cakes.

□ Fresh mint leaves make a delicious addition to freshly cooked vegetables, especially potatoes and peas.

Pennyroyal (M. pulegium) →

□ Mint may be used sparingly in soups, stuffings and marinades.

□ Try mixing finely chopped mint leaves with sugar and sprinkling on chilled watermelon just before serving.

Corn mint

Cape velvet mint

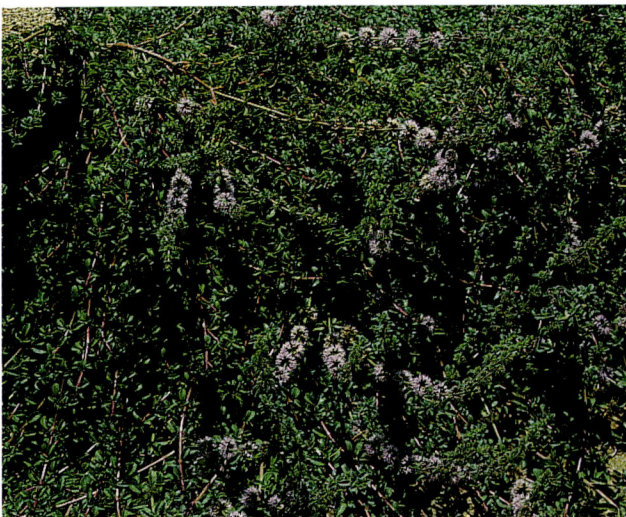

MUSTARD/MOSTERD
Brassica alba, B. negra
Family: Cruciferae

Mustard is indigenous to Europe, Asia Minor, China, North and South America, North Africa and western India. It has had a multitude of uses since prehistoric times – medicinal as well as culinary. In fact in the first century AD Pliny listed 40 remedies containing mustard. The name derives from the Roman word "mustus," the new wine they mixed with the seed, and "ardens," meaning "fiery." The Romans believed that the herb has an aphrodisiac effect.

Today ground mustard powder is found on kitchen shelves throughout the world. Almost every type of sauce, vinegar, chutney and savoury dish requires a dash of mustard. Although most people buy their mustard from shops, it is an easy herb to grow and very worthwhile to make your own mustard.

CULTIVATION
Mustard is very easy to cultivate and in view of its culinary importance should be seen as an essential part of a herb garden. It is a hardy annual.

Conditions: Mustard likes a sunny spot, with fertile and well-drained soil, with some shade in summer.

Propagation: You can grow mustard sprouts by sprinkling the seeds over a tray lined with damp cotton wool or thick lint. Keep them moist and within three days the seeds will have sprouted. When they are about 5 cm in height cut them off at the roots to use in cooking. When one tray sprouts you can start another, so that you always have fresh shoots to use as salad greens and for cooking. Sow seeds in spring for a seed crop. Dig over a bed and add some manure and compost, about a spadeful of each to an area 1 m square. Sow the seeds thinly, rake over and water well. The plants will appear within ten days.

Containers: Grow sprouts in trays as described above.

Size: The plant grows to 30-90 cm.

Harvesting: The flowers, which are edible, can be picked as they open, but the seed pods should be picked before they open. The sprouts are usually ready 8-10 days after sowing.

Dos and don'ts: Don't plant mustard next to cabbages and cauliflowers – they will become an aphid playground. Do plant mustard as a green manure crop in depleted soil. Dig it in once it flowers, and leave until spring.

USES
Domestic
☐ To clean very dirty pots, put in a few bruised mustard seeds, add a little water and vinegar, stand overnight and rinse well the next day.

Cosmetic
☐ Pulverised mustard seeds can be rubbed onto the hands as a deodoriser. Rinse off after a few minutes. Take care with tender skins!

Medicinal
☐ Mustard is used in the treatment of flatulence, poor appetite, colds, catarrh, chest and bladder ailments.

☐ Mustard seeds and leaves have long been used to make a poultice for rheumatism, sprains and chilblains. Mustard can also be added to footbaths to aid circulation and relieve fatigue. A mustard plaster can be made by mixing a handful of crushed seeds with a handful of wholewheat flower into a paste, using hot water. Add two tablespoons of vinegar. Spread on a cloth and apply hot over the area to be treated. Where the skin is sensitive, add the beaten white of an egg to the mixture and test a small area of skin first.

☐ Mustard is an emetic, i.e. it encourages vomiting.

☐ Chewing mustard leaves will help ward off a cold.

Culinary
☐ Make your own mustard by gathering mustard seed from your garden and grinding it to a paste, adding cider vinegar and a little honey. Black mustard seeds have the strongest flavour but the brown ones are easier to harvest and the white ones last the longest.

☐ Mustard powder is widely used as a condiment for savoury dishes, and mustard seeds are commonly used in preserves, pickles and chutneys.

☐ Fresh mustard sprouts can be served in salads, sprinkled over roasts or floated in soup.

☐ Use mustard flowers in salads and on sandwiches.

☐ The fresh leaves, finely chopped, can be added to salads and combined with chopped celery, avocado pear, parsley and chopped sorrel leaves to make an exceptionally tasty green salad.

MYRTLE/MIRT
Myrtus communis
Family: Myrtaceae

Myrtle is a very ancient herb, having been mentioned in the Old Testament and in the works of the ancient Greeks and Romans. It is named after Myrrha, who was a favourite priestess of Venus, the goddess of love, who turned her into a myrtle bush to protect her from an over-eager suitor. It is considered to be lucky and in some countries is carried by brides in their wedding bouquets for harmony, faithfulness and many children! It is dedicated to Venus and is said to have an aphrodisiac effect. The plant is highly scented and has attractive pure white flowers with golden stamens. A myrtle crown is a Christmas blessing worn by children lighting church candles in some countries.

CULTIVATION
Myrtle is a perennial shrub that grows slowly and requires little attention apart from the occasional trim.
Conditions: Myrtle likes a medium rich, well-drained soil and a sunny situation.
Propagation: With woody cuttings. Choose woody twigs in midsummer, pull off with a small "heel" and strip lower leaves. Press into trays filled with a mixture of peat and sand. Cover with a plastic tent and keep moist until rooted. Then remove the plastic and allow to establish strongly before planting in bags filled with compost and soil. Place the bags in a partially shaded position and do not allow them to dry out, but do not overwater. Once sturdy and strong plant out 1 to 2 m apart in well-dug holes to which a little compost has been added (one spadeful per plant). Water well until established and then once a week.
Size: Grows up to 3 m high.
Harvesting: Ripe berries, buds and flowers can be picked whenever available. Pick leaves when the plant is in flower for stronger scent.
Dos and don'ts: In the hot weather give the plants a spray of water to keep their leaves looking shiny.

USES
Domestic
☐ The myrtle branch is ideal for making wreaths.
☐ The leaves and flowers make a fragrant addition to potpourris and sachets, and the dried berries are excellent potpourri fixatives.

Cosmetic
☐ The myrtle berry can be used to make a rinse for dark hair. The berries can be dried for use throughout the year. To make the rinse boil a cupful of dry berries in 2 litres of water. Cool and strain. Alternatively pour a litre of boiling water over a cup of fresh ripe berries and stand until cool, then strain.
☐ Myrtle is astringent and antiseptic and a brew made as described above can be applied to the face to tighten pores and tone the complexion. Use the brew on pads of cotton wool – save any excess and store in the fridge.

Medicinal
☐ A brew can be made from myrtle leaves to soothe bruises and haemorrhoids and as a douche for vaginal discharges. Pour a litre of boiling water over two cups of leaves, and allow to stand for an hour. Strain then dip a cotton cloth into the brew, wring it out and bind it over the bruised area. Apply several times a day.
☐ A brew made by pouring a cup of boiling water over a tablespoon of fresh myrtle leaves and flowers, then left to stand for five minutes and strained, can be drunk to relive psoriasis and sinusitis. It can also be splashed onto the skin to ease itchiness.
☐ You can make a refreshing myrtle vinegar to use in the bath by heating a litre of apple cider vinegar with a cup of myrtle leaves and flowers, a cup of rosemary twigs and 10 cloves. Bring to the boil, simmer for 5 minutes then remove from the stove and allow to steep and cool. Strain off the vinegar and bottle, adding a fresh sprig of rosemary and one of myrtle. Just two or three tablespoons in your evening bath will do wonders for aching muscles and fatigue.

Culinary
☐ The dried flower buds and the berrylike myrtle fruit can be crushed and used instead of peppercorns.
☐ Sprinkle a handful of leaves over a pork roast in the last ten minutes of roasting to enhance the flavour.
☐ Add fresh myrtle flowers to salads and fruit salads. Remove the tough calyx and sprinkle the petals.

NASTURTIUM/KAPPERTJIE
Tropaeolum majus, T. minus
Family: Tropaeolaceae

Nasturtium (T. majus)

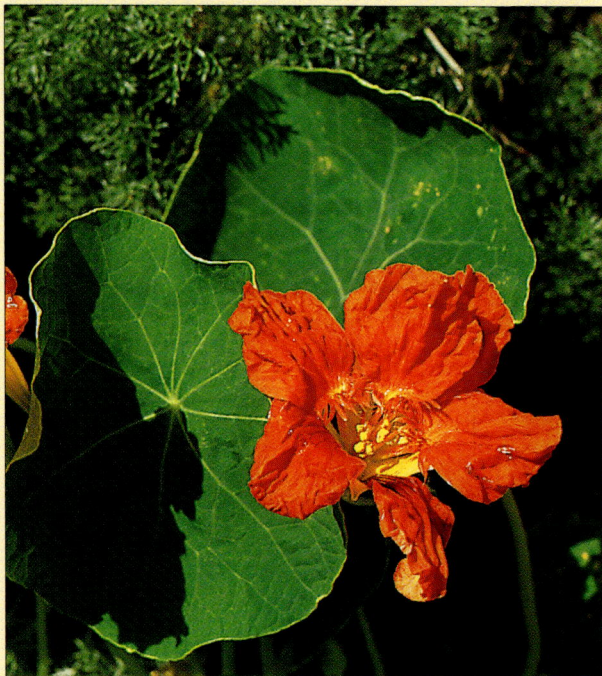

There are many different varieties of nasturtiums. Some are climbers, some semi-trailers and some dwarfs. They all have colourful flowers, usually in red, yellow or orange. The scientific name derives from the Greek word "tropaion," meaning "trophy." It is so called because the flower and leaf look like the helmet and shield of the trophies with which many ancient monuments were decorated. Tropaeolum majus has long, trailing stems and is known as the common nasturtium, whereas T. minus is a compact, bushy herb that grows to a height and width of about 30 cm.

CULTIVATION
The nasturtium is a hardy annual plant.
Conditions: Likes sandy soil and a sunny position, but can survive in most soil types.
Propagation: From seeds. Sow seeds in spring 40 cm apart where they are to flower, and keep damp. In frost-free areas nasturtiums are self-seeding and even sometimes perennial. When preparing a bed for nasturtiums, dig in a generous amount of well-rotted manure and compost and sow the seeds in moist, friable soil. Keep well watered until mature then water once a week.
Size: 37 cm (trailing); 30 cm otherwise.

Harvesting: Pick leaves and flowers as required; seeds when ripe.
Dos and don'ts: If planted near broccoli, nasturtium keeps it free from aphids. It keeps woolly aphids away from apple trees. It makes a superb companion plant to mealies, tomatoes and cabbages.

USES
Domestic
☐ Crushed nasturtium seeds can be added to insect repelling sprays. The seeds can be harvested all year round and stored in vinegar for future use.

Cosmetic
☐ Crushed nasturtium petals placed on pimples help to soothe and heal them, and crushed leaves and flowers in aqueous cream relieve cracked heels.

Medicinal
☐ Nasturtium leaves are high in vitamin C and are effective in treating sore throats. Chew one at the first sign of soreness and then another every 2 or 3 hours.
☐ Nasturtium has natural antibiotic qualities and is an aid to digestion, nerves and depression. It can also be used to cure loss of appetite and fatigue.
☐ An infusion can be made by steeping a quarter cup of fresh leaves in a cup of boiling water for five minutes. Strain and drink a sherry glass two or three times a day to relieve chronic bronchitis, bronchial catarrh and emphysema. It will also help chronic coughs.
☐ The leaves and juices from the stems are used in the treatment of chronic sores (applied locally), cystitis and inflammation of the kidneys. Bind leaves and stems over the affected part and leave overnight.
☐ A poultice may be made of crushed nasturtium seeds placed on a bandage then wrung out in hot water. Apply to boils, abscesses, sties and sores twice daily.
☐ To treat colic or digestive gripings, grind a teaspoon of seeds and dissolve in enough water to liquefy, then give to the sufferer every three hours.

Culinary
☐ The leaves and the flowers have a cresslike taste and can be used in green salads and as a sandwich filling (especially tasty when mixed with cream cheese).
☐ The flowers make an attractive garnish for food and look particularly good when floated in a punchbowl or used to decorate savoury dishes and salads.
☐ Nasturtium seeds have a strong, peppery flavour and can be used in sauces or pickled, in which case they taste like capers. To pickle, pack seeds into a bottle with a sprig of thyme, a few cloves and two bay leaves. Cover with hot vinegar and a sprinkling of salt. Seal and store for a month before use.

ONION/UI
Allium cepa
Family: Liliaceae

The onion has been cultivated for at least 2 000 years. It is probably native to central Asia or India but is now grown worldwide. It contains a wide range of vitamins and has undoubted medicinal properties, but of course is best known for its versatility in cooking. The onion is perhaps the most widely used of all vegetables, with the advantage of being generally available all year round.

Use of the plant was recorded by the ancient Egyptians, Chaldeans and Greeks. There are numerous cultivars of A. cepa, including shallots, spring onions, tree onions, Welsh onions, scallions, everready onions and chives.

CULTIVATION
Many of the onions are hardy perennials, but the "domestic" onion is an annual.

Conditions: The onion plant likes a sunny position. It thrives in a rich soil that is moist but well drained.

Propagation: Sow seed in trays and transplant when seedlings are 6 cm high, into rows 20 cm apart.

Size: The onion plant grows to a height of between 20 and 30 cm.

Harvesting: Once the leaves begin to dry, pull the plants up and tie in bundles, store in a cool place and use as required, pulling off individual onions from the bundle.

Dos and don'ts: Onions grow well with beetroot, and their growth is promoted by placing them near chamomile. Alternate rows of carrots and onions will protect the carrots from carrot fly.

USES
Domestic
☐ Onion skins can be used to make a yellow dye.

☐ A spray for potato and tomato blight can be made from chopped garlic and onions. Chop 2 bulbs of garlic and 4 large onions, boil with 3 litres of water, then cool and strain. Use soon after preparation.

☐ A sliced onion placed in a sickroom will absorb germs. Replace with fresh slices daily and thereafter burn the old ones.

Cosmetic
☐ A slice of onion heals cuts and acne, and in the diet promotes hair growth.

☐ Rubbing the scalp with chopped onion is said to promote hair growth. Leave on for 15 minutes, wash hair with a mild shampoo and follow with a vinegar rinse.

Medicinal
☐ The onion contains vitamins A, B1, B2, B3, C and E. It has antibiotic properties and is diuretic, antispasmodic, hypotensive and hypoglycaemic. It also reduces blood pressure and blood sugar levels and is useful in treating coughs, colds, bronchitis and gastric complaints.

☐ Onion juice can be used to treat cuts and grazes, as well as acne.

☐ Laryngitis or sore throats can be treated by using the old folk remedy of binding onion slices around the throat.

☐ Half a warm, baked onion can be applied to a boil to bring it to a head.

☐ Onion juice can be applied to wasp and bee stings to soothe them.

☐ The juice of one medium onion (extracted in a garlic press) can be added to half a cup of chopped pennyroyal mint and 250 ml boiling water to make a gout cure. Pour the boiling water over the pennyroyal and stand for 20 minutes, then strain and add the onion juice. Dip a piece of lint into the mixture and wrap it around the afflicted area. Eating onions can also help to relieve gout.

Culinary
☐ Onions are widely used in soups, stews, meat and poultry dishes, and raw in salads. They make the breath rather smelly, particularly if eaten raw, but this can be avoided by chewing a sprig of parsley or a couple of cloves after eating onions.

☐ All cultivars of *A. cepa* have culinary uses, particularly in savoury dishes, pickles and marinades.

☐ Onions are delicious on their own when fried, either plain or in batter.

OREGANO (OREGANUM)/OREGO
Origanum vulgare
Family: Labiatae

Golden creeping oregano

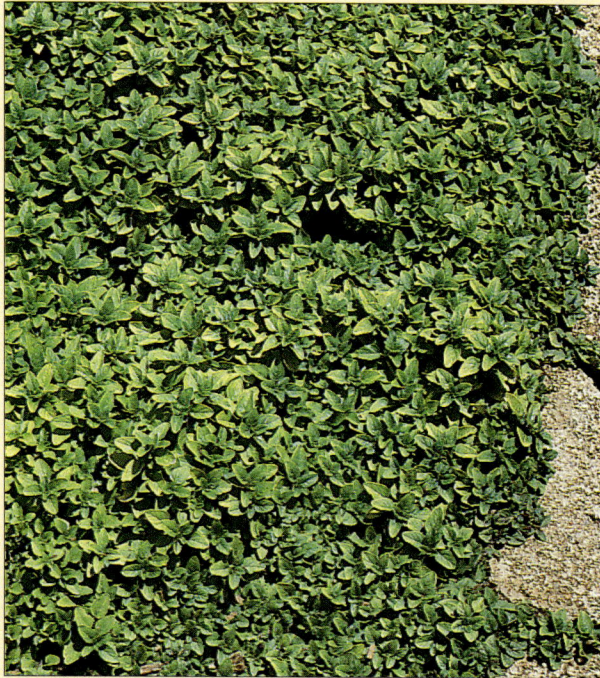

The name of this ancient herb is said to derive from the Greek words "oros ganos," meaning "joy of the mountain." There is another theory that says that Oregano, a young servant of King Cinyras of Crete, was carrying a large vessel of expensive perfume when he tripped and spilled the precious liquid. He was so shocked that he fainted, and while lying on the ground he was changed into the fragrant oregano plant, absorbing some of the spilled perfume's fragrance. It is also known as wild marjoram and is closely related to marjoram. It has been prized for its healing, disinfectant and preserving properties at least since the days of ancient Egypt. The creeping variety has pinkish flowers and the bush type has small white flowers.

CULTIVATION
Oregano is a creeping perennial.
Conditions: Likes sun and average soil.
Propagation: By seeds or cuttings. The seeds are slow to germinate; as cuttings root easily it is more satisfactory to propagate this way. Take cuttings at any time of year and press into wet sand. Keep moist and shaded. Harden off by standing the tray in the sun for a few days before transplanting. Water twice a week and leave 30 to 50 cm between plants. Cut well back to discourage straggliness. The creeping variety spreads by runners that root easily, so if required these can be cut away and transplanted into another position.

Containers: Oregano makes a good container plant. It needs sun, so make sure it is in a sunny position.
Size: Up to 30 cm.
Harvesting: Harvest any time of year – oregano withstands winter frosts well, so is evergreen all year.
Dos and don'ts: The creeping varieties make excellent edgings to paths and trouble-free ground covers. They all benefit from pruning.

USES
Domestic
☐ The strong oils in all varieties of oregano are much disliked by all insects, so it is ideal to add to insect repelling sprays.
☐ Rub on furniture to sweeten a room after smokers have been in it.

Cosmetic
☐ Oregano leaf can be put in a bath for an invigorating effect. Tie a handful in a muslin square and use with soap to give elbows, knees and feet a brisk rub – it sloughs off old skin cells.
☐ Make a strong infusion of oregano leaves to use as a hair conditioner and growth stimulant. Boil a cup of fresh leaves in 1 *l* of water (preferably rain water) for 15 minutes. Cool and strain, then comb and massage into the hair.

Medicinal
☐ Oregano can be used to make a tea to treat coughs, nervous headaches and irritability, tiredness and stomach and gallbladder disorders. It is also said to be effective in treating seasickness and menstrual cramps. Make the standard brew by pouring a cup of boiling water over a quarter cup of fresh leaves. Stand for 5 minutes and strain.
☐ Apply the flowering top externally as a poultice for swellings, rheumatism and stiff necks. Mash it in hot water and place on a crêpe bandage.
☐ Oregano leaves can be chewed, or the essential oil applied, to relieve toothache.

Culinary
☐ Oregano is an essential ingredient in pizzas and other Italian dishes, and goes well with tomatoes, lamb, egg and cheese dishes.
☐ Use fresh oregano sparingly in salads.
☐ Oregano has the ability to dissolve fats in the body, so it is an excellent addition to fatty meat dishes like pork. Sprinkle half a cup of chopped oregano over the meat while it is roasting. Sprinkle over chips and fritters, and add to gravies and sauces.
☐ A little oregano added to stir fries gives an excitingly fresh taste.
☐ Dried oregano added to coarsely ground black pepper, sea salt and a touch of thinly grated lemon peel is a superb flavour enhancer for hams, sausages and pork dishes.

PYRETHRUM/KWYLWORTEL
Chrysanthemum cinerarifolium
Family: Compositae

This plant, with its lovely daisy-like flowers, deserves a prominent place in the garden. It is the source of a natural insecticide, once grown extensively in Kenya, and is still commercially cultivated for this purpose. Pyrethrum originated in Persia and the Caucasus and was once the prime crop of Dalmatia – hence its alternative name Dalmatian daisy.

CULTIVATION

Pyrethrum is a hardy herbaceous perennial plant. It grows easily and produces a lovely long-flowering garden flower which also lasts well in vases. The flowers are harmless to humans but are used as an insecticide when dried, flowers, powdered or as a tincture diluted with water in the ratio of one part to ten. This was once much sought after as an insect repellent, particularly effective against mosquitoes.

Conditions: The plant likes a light, well-drained soil and full sun.

Propagation: From seeds. Sow them in sand-filled trays, cover with a fine layer of sand and keep moist. When seedlings are big enough to handle transplant them into a well-dug bed to which some river sand has been added. Space 30 cm apart and keep well watered at first. Once the plant is growing well water every 2 or 3 days as the soil does not retain moisture for long. It benefits from a mulch of leaves and grass to retain moisture once it has established itself, especially in very hot areas. Seed can also be sown where it is to grow and thinned out when it germinates. Make sure the seed bed is shady and moist, using hessian to cover it if necessary. Keep the sides enclosed too as wind dries out the sandy soil. The thinned out plants can be transplanted while the plant is still young. The plants live for about six years on average.

Size: The plant grows to 75 cm.

Harvesting: After the summer flowering cut back the flowering stalks.

Dos and don'ts: Do alternate rows of pyrethrum plants with tomatoes and beans to keep pests away. Use it as a border around the rose garden to deter aphids.

USES

Domestic

☐ Pyrethrum flowers are the source of a natural insecticide, pyrethrin, that is commercially exploited in South Africa and Kenya, among other places.

☐ The heads can be dried and used in potpourris, and will give the added benefit of keeping insects away. A muslin bag can be filled with leaves and flowers and hung on a dog's basket to repel fleas and ticks. The flowers and leaves should be replaced from time to time. Dried pyrethrum flowers can be placed behind rows of books to keep fish moths away. Pyrethrum is quite harmless to mammals so can be used generously. Crush flowers and leaves to sprinkle on stored fruit and vegetables and in grain bags.

☐ The pyrethrum flower can also be made into a liquid insecticide spray. Add a quarter bucket of dried, crushed pyrethrum flowers to half a bucket of khakibos, half a bucket of wilde als, basil or southernwood (or a mixture of all three), and cover the herbs with boiling water. Cool overnight and strain, then add another bucket of water and 2 cups of soap powder and 2 cups of ash from a wood fire. Mix well and splash on plants, or use as a spray on scale aphids, red spider, etc.

☐ Use the pruned end-of-summer flowers in sprays and add to compost.

PARSLEY/PIETERSIELIE

Petroselinum crispum

Family: Umbelliferae

Moss curled parsley

Known as the king of herbs, parsley has been used since time immemorial. It was held in particularly high esteem by the ancient Greeks, who associated it with Archemorus, the herald of death. For this reason they used it to decorate tombs.

Parsley has been used medicinally for thousands of years, but it only really came into its own as a culinary herb in Roman times, when it was widely consumed. Today parsley is the most common of garnishes and probably the most versatile herb from a culinary point of view. It is one herb that no discerning cook can afford to be without! The flat-leafed parsleys, such as the Italian and Greek varieties, can be used in the same way as the common parsley.

CULTIVATION

Most herb gardens have a parsley plant or two, and it's sure to be the most commonly used plant in the garden. It is a hardy biennial.

Conditions: Parsley likes a rich moist soil and full sun, but can be grown in semi-filtered shade, or morning sun and afternoon shade, if you live in a hot part of the country. Keep the soil fairly moist and dig in a lot of compost throughout the summer. The flowering period can be postponed by picking the leaves often and cutting down the flowering stems.

Propagation: This is best done by seed. The plants grow slowly, so if you're impatient buy a tray of seedlings from the nursery. If sowing your own, do so in early spring. Soak the seed in warm (not hot) water in a thermos overnight and then sow into sand-filled trays. Prepare the trays by soaking them in water and then covering finely with sand. Place a sheet of glass over the tray and keep it in the shade. Once the seed has sprouted the glass can be removed and the trays kept moist. Transplant 15-20 cm apart when you can handle the plants and keep them shaded with hessian or cloches for a few days.

Containers: Parsley can be grown in pots if desired, but it needs full sun.

Size: Grows to 15-25 cm.

Harvesting: Pick the leaves at any time. Collect the seeds when ripe. To prolong the plant's life cut off the flowering head.

Dos and don'ts: Do grow parsley near roses and tomatoes to keep them free of insects and diseases. Parsley looks charming as an edging plant! It will attract bees to your garden.

USES

Domestic

☐ Dried parsley leaves can be used to make a natural green dye.

Cosmetic

☐ Parsley can be added to the boiling water used for steaming the face. An infusion can be applied to the skin to minimise freckles, or used as an eye bath.

☐ A lotion made of parsley leaves and seeds and rubbed into the scalp will remove dandruff, stimulate hair growth, check baldness and get rid of lice. It is definitely the hairdresser's best ally!

Medicinal

☐ Chew fresh parsley leaves to sweeten the breath after eating garlic or onions.

☐ Parsley tea, made from the fresh leaves, can be used to treat kidney and bladder infections and flatulence, and also as a slimming aid. Make it by pouring a cup of boiling water over a quarter cup of fresh leaves; leave to stand for 5 minutes and strain. Never take more than 1 cup a day, for no more than five days running.

☐ Many people believe that parsley can be effective against rheumatism if the sufferer drinks a glass of parsley tea a day. Parsley tea is also excellent for diabetics, but do not take it for longer than 5 days, breaking off for 3 to 5 days and then continuing.

☐ Parsley stimulates the appetite, so it is an ideal dietary supplement for invalids or old people who find eating difficult.

☐ Parsley tea is also effective in combating "female complaints" such as cystitis, kidney infections, excessive and painful menstruation.

☐ When weaning an infant, parsley leaves worn inside the brassiere will dry up the milk. Bruised leaves, steeped in vinegar, will also soothe painful swollen breasts.

☐ Warmed crushed parsley leaves and seeds will relieve insect stings.

☐ Parsley is gaining recognition in the treatment of cancer and some herbalists recommend that people from families with a history of the disease eat the herb as a preventive measure.

☐ Parsley is effective against jaundice, rickets, anaemia, arthritis and sciatica. Half a cup of leaves should be eaten by sufferers daily and a strong tea drunk once daily. Make the tea as described above.

Culinary

☐ Besides having a delightful taste parsley is extremely nutritious. It is well known as a garnish and can be used in soups and stews, sprinkled onto vegetables and mixed into cream cheese. Add it to cooked vegetables and stews just before serving as it is at its best uncooked. In fact, parsley can be used to add a special touch to almost any dish.

☐ Parsley dries beautifully and can be used in bouquet garni.

Flat leaf parsley

☐ The root of the plant can be used in bouquet garni or boiled as a root vegetable.

Parsley eggs

This is a tasty change from ordinary fried eggs and is a quick and easy supper or breakfast dish.

3 tablespoons butter
4 fresh eggs
salt, pepper
1 large onion, sliced into rings
2 tablespoons chopped parsley
1 clove garlic, finely chopped

Melt the butter in a heavy-bottomed saucepan. Break the eggs into the pan and fry gently. Lift out onto a hot serving dish, sprinkle with salt and pepper and keep hot.

Fry the onion rings, adding more butter if necessary. (Alternatively, dip the onion rings into a light batter and fry them in oil.) Lift out and drain. Keep hot.

Mix the rest of the butter with the chopped parsley and garlic and a little salt. Drop this in small lumps over the hot eggs. Serve immediately with hot toast and a salad.

The garlic parsley butter is so popular that I make a double quantity to spread on toast.

SERVES 4

Parsley potted cheese

This is a most delicious spread. It is nourishing and tasty and can be used as a sandwich filling, a pastry case filling or for savoury tarts.

1 cup butter
1 cup coarsely grated mozzarella cheese
2 cups coarsely grated Cheddar cheese
1 egg, beaten
$1/2 - 3/4$ cup medium sweet sherry
little pepper
1 heaped tablespoon fresh thyme or marjoram
1 heaped tablespoon fresh chives
3 heaped tablespoons parsley, finely chopped
$1/2$ teaspoon dried mace

Melt butter and cheese over a double boiler and add the egg. Beat well and remove from heat. Beat in sherry, pepper and herbs. Press into small pots, cover with melted butter and tin foil. Refrigerate and decorate with a sprig of parsley before serving.

PELARGONIUM (SCENTED GERANIUMS)/MALVA

Pelargonium species
Family: Geraniaceae

Rose-scented geranium (P. graveolens)

There are many species of fragrant geraniums, and they are an asset to any garden, not just for their lovely smell but because of the bright, cheerful flowers. They also have culinary and medicinal uses. They vary in height from a few centimetres (P. fragrans, also known as the nutmeg geranium), to the rose-scented P. graveolens, a tall plant. Because they are indigenous to South Africa they are easy to grow and no garden should be without at least one or two scented geraniums. The typical pelargonium has five petals, two of which are broader than the other three, giving it its distinctive asymmetrical appearance, and it is this arrangement of petals that distinguishes pelargoniums from true geraniums. The pelargoniums were introduced to Europe by voyagers who called at the Cape in the 1600s (it reached Britain in 1632), before the European settlement had even been founded at the Cape. They are now well established overseas, and a worldwide favourite. The Khoikhoi (Hottentots) used the leaves of scented geranium to make poultices, teas and medicines and when the white settlers first arrived in South Africa they adopted the use of this very versatile medicinal plant.

CULTIVATION

The pelargonium is a tender evergreen perennial.
Conditions: Pelargoniums like a sunny exposure, but in very hot areas they benefit from partial shade. They grow well in average soil that is well drained.

Propagation: Cuttings, sometimes seeds. Cuttings can be taken any time of year except the coldest months. Choose a compact side shoot about 10 cm long and pull off a small "heel." Remove the lower leaves and preferably dip into rooting hormone, then press into wet sand. Keep protected and damp until rooted. In colder areas take cuttings at the end of April. Stand boxes in a protected place, make a frame over them and cover with plastic. Wait until spring has definitely set in before planting out as they are very susceptible to frost. Plant 90 cm apart as the rose-scented varieties grow very quickly.

Containers: They make ideal indoor plants, but they do like full sun. As they do not like frost they can be transplanted into pots and brought inside in winter.

Size: Pelargoniums grow to a height of 15 to 120 cm, depending on species.

Harvesting: Pick leaves when required because if the plant is well composted it will soon replace them.

Dos and don'ts: Do plant pelargoniums as hedging plants. Do keep them well trimmed as they tend to become untidy. Do protect them with grass in frosty areas. They are very drought resistant and benefit from being constantly pruned, particularly *P. graveolens*.

USES

Domestic

☐ The leaves are a fragrant ingredient in potpourri.

☐ Rub scented geranium leaves into greasy or paint stained hands; they remove the dirt very effectively.

☐ Rub wooden furniture with the leaves of the rose-scented geranium; it imparts a lovely fragrance that will last a long time.

Cosmetic

☐ Oil of rose-scented geranium is used in the perfume industry.

☐ The essential oil can be added to face creams, and is useful in balancing the sebum in oily and dry or inflamed skin. An infusion of the leaf can be used as a mild astringent to cleanse and improve circulation. Also add to bath water, and make an infusion of the leaves for rinsing greasy hair after shampooing.

Medicinal

☐ There are so many varieties of pelargonium, and so many different medicinal applications, that it is impossible to list them all here. Refer to *Indigenous Healing Plants* by Margaret Roberts (Southern Books, 1990) for full details.

☐ An infusion of the leaves is effective against dysentery and diarrhoea. Take 5 leaves of *P. graveolens* or the hooded geranium *P. cuculatum* and steep in 250 ml boiling water, then stand for 5 minutes and strain. Take one tablespoonful every half hour until the condition eases.

☐ The essential oil is used in aromatherapy massages and benefits premenstrual tension, fluid retention, eczema, dermatitis and dry skin.

☐ The scented geraniums, particularly *P. graveolens*, are well known anti-tension herbs and aid sleep and relaxation, as well as soothe the digestion. A pillow stuffed with the fragrant leaves is a great aid to sleep.

☐ As its name suggests, camphor leaf geranium (*P. betulinum*) smells like camphor and can be used to clear coughs, stuffy noses and chest ailments. Infuse leaves in boiling water and inhale the camphor-scented steam.

☐ The sap of the ivy-leaved geranium (*P. peltatum*) has been used to relieve sore throats, and an infusion of the petals in hot water (I tablespoonful of petals to 1 cup water), applied to the skin with cotton wool, has an astringent effect.

Culinary

☐ The flowers can be tossed in salads.

☐ The leaves can be used as a flavouring for food and drinks. A few leaves at the bottom of the pan when baking cakes and custards will leave a lovely taste and fragrance. They can also be added to cooldrinks and jellies for the same reason. Other dishes that benefit from a dash of pelargonium leaf include liver pâté and jams.

☐ The flavour of the leaves combines well with ginger and vanilla.

☐ The peppermint geranium, *P. tomentosum*, is particularly delicious in drinks.

☐ Apple geranium, *P. odoratissimum*, smells and tastes like apples and is delicious added to apple dishes.

☐ *P. limonseum* has a lemony scent and is widely used for baked puddings and jellies.

Rose-scented geranium scones
3 cups cake flour
1 cup Nuttiwheat flour
250 g butter
2 tablespoons chopped scented geranium leaves
4 tablespoons sugar (optional)
1 teaspoon salt
8 teaspoons baking powder
1¹/2 cups milk

Rub butter into dry ingredients. Add chopped scented geranium. Mix in milk to make a fairly soft dough. Turn out dough onto a floured surface, pat out to about 2 cm in height. Cut out shapes. Bake at 200 °C for about 15 minutes until light brown

MAKES 1 DOZEN

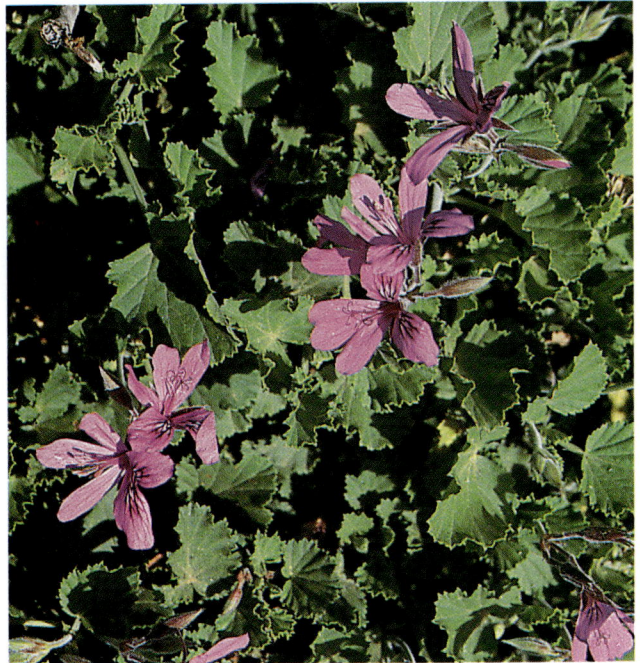

Camphor leaf geranium (P. betulinum)

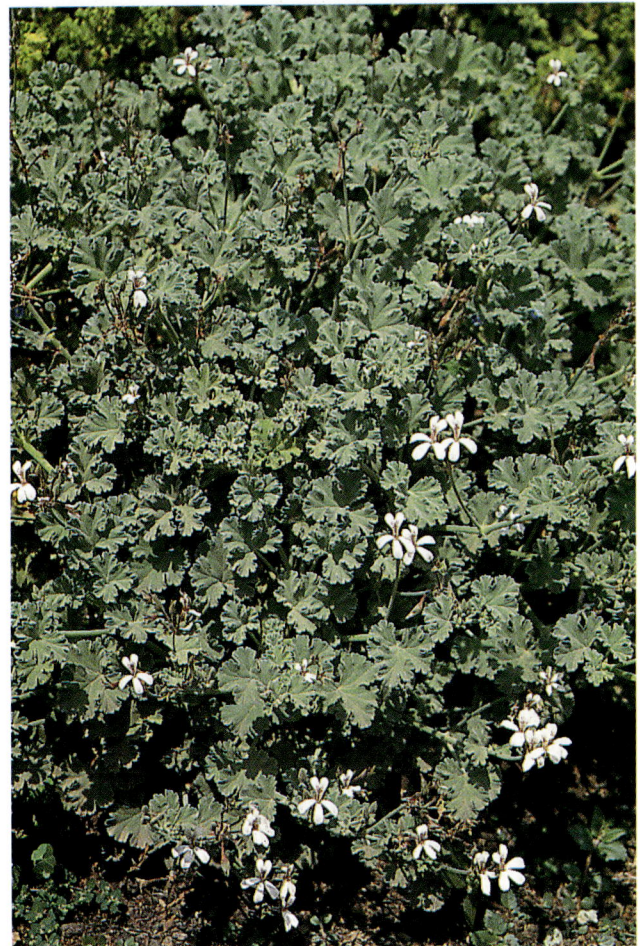

Nutmeg geranium (P. fragrans)

ROCKET/MOSTERDSLAAI
Eruca vesicaria
Family: Cruciferae

Rocket is a new herb to many people, as it was only introduced to South Africa a few years ago.
However it has been a favourite in Europe, particularly in the Mediterranean regions, for several centuries. It was hailed as an excellent remedy for scurvy in the 16th century.

CULTIVATION
Rocket is a biennial which grows very easily and abundantly under a variety of conditions.
Conditions: Needs full sun and richly composted soil. Withstands frost, cold winds, summer storms and summer heat.
Size: Grows to between 50 cm and 1 m.
Harvesting: Pick young leaves and flowers for use in salads. Older leaves can be used in soups and stews.
Dos and don'ts: Rocket can be grown in a deep pot – make sure that the soil is well composted, water it daily and position in the full sun.

USES
Domestic
☐ Rocket is a remarkable plant food: I mix it with comfrey or borage and water it onto precious plants.
☐ Plant rocket as a "green manure" crop where you have grown vegetables, dig it into the soil and leave the ground fallow for two months.
☐ Add rocket leaves to the compost heap, as it breaks down quickly. Better still plant rocket around your compost heap and it will seed itself continuously.

Cosmetic
☐ Rocket is an astringent and makes a very refreshing foot bath (once you get used to the strong smell).

Medicinal
☐ It is a digestive which help cleanse the body of pollutants.
☐ In the country districts of Italy rocket leaves are boiled in honey to make a cough syrup.
☐ Rocket should be included in the diet to help anaemia, digestive upsets, fluid retention, bladder ailments, malnutrition, scurvy and vitamin deficiencies.

Culinary
☐ Rocket has a rich meaty and mustardy flavour.
☐ It is rich in iron, chlorophyll and vitamins and is a famed antiscorbutic which makes it a very valuable food.
☐ A delicious addition to salads.
☐ Add to any soup or stew – it is particularly good with tomatoes or split peas.

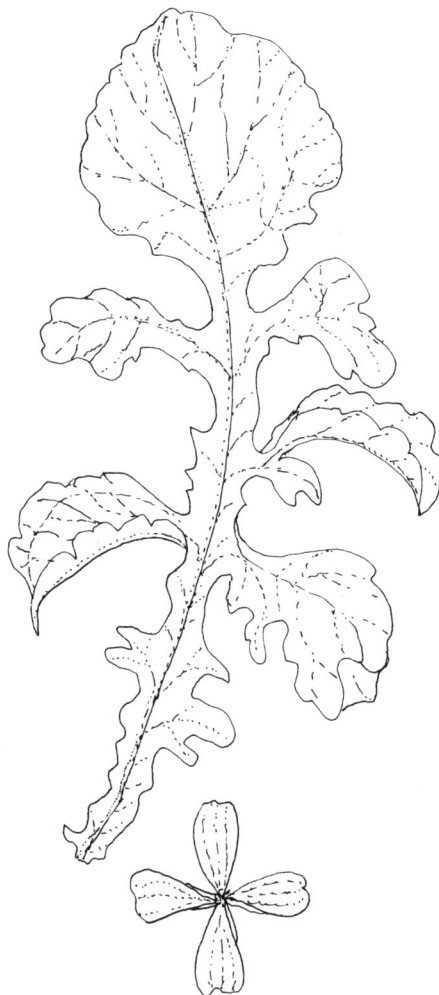

ROSE/ROOS
Rosa species
Family: Rosaceae

Crimson glory

The rose is not strictly speaking a herb but deserves a place in every garden not only because of its beauty and scent but also for its medicinal properties. The old herb gardens all featured the cabbage rose, R. centifolia, but it went out of fashion a long time ago. Some nurseries have begun to stock the old roses, however. There are so many varieties of roses that a choice must be subject to personal preference. Most rose varieties can be used for cosmetic, culinary and medicinal purposes – my favourite is Crimson Glory, and the newly developed centifolia rose: "the Margaret Roberts rose."

CULTIVATION

The rose is a perennial shrub.

Conditions: Roses like an average soil and a sunny situation.

Propagation: By cuttings. These should be taken from a strong flowering stem when the bloom has faded. Cut the flower off and divide the stem into lengths with 3 or 4 eyes on each piece. Press halfway into wet sand and keep watered and cool until new shoots appear. Then strengthen by exposing to the sun for longer periods each day. Plant out into bags so that they can become well established before transplanting in the garden. Space about 120 cm apart. Dig a hole 60 cm by 45 cm for each plant. Make a mound in the centre and stand the rose in it, spreading its roots out. cover with soil, press well down and water liberally. This is usually done in July, as is the pruning. Do not put manure or compost in the hole; rather mulch with coarse compost once the plant is established, and water weekly.

Size: Varies according to species, up to about 3 m. Some varieties are climbers.

Harvesting: Cut flowers just before they are in full bloom. Petals can also be dried.

Dos and don'ts: If you want to grow a climbing rose, make sure that the support is in place before you plant the rose or the roots may be damaged when you dig holes for trellises or other supports. Roses need a good watering programme and regular checking for insect infestation. Grow insect repelling herbs like catmint (*Nepeta mussinii* – the small-leafed variety), winter savory, creeping rosemary or pennyroyal under roses.

USES

Domestic
☐ The rose is one of the most popular and attractive cut flowers for vase arrangements.
☐ The dried petals are an essential ingredient in pot-pourri.

Cosmetic
☐ Rosewater is very beneficial to the skin, as it has an antiseptic, soothing quality. It may be used even on sensitive and inflamed skins. Rosewater can be made by boiling 2 cups of petals in 2 cups of water for 15 minutes. Cool and strain. Keep excess in the fridge.

Medicinal
☐ Rose petal tea has a calming, tranquillising effect. Make it by pouring a cup of boiling water over a quarter cup of rose petals; leave to stand for 5 minutes and strain. Serve with honey if desired.
☐ Rose oil is used as a massage oil. It is said to aid circulation and tone the blood capillaries.
☐ Rosewater may be splashed on the outside of the eyes in cases of conjunctivitis.
☐ The rosehip contains several vitamins and is particularly rich in vitamin C. It can be taken in the form of a tea or syrup.

Culinary
☐ The petals are used to make rose petal conserve and to flavour ice-cream. The bitter white heel of the petal should be removed before use.

ROSEMARY/ROOSMARYN
Rosmarinus officinalis
Family: Labiatae

Rosemary is one of the most ancient of herbs, and its use has been recorded since the earliest times. The leaf, branch, stem, flowers and seeds have a multitude of medicinal and culinary uses, and the herb is particularly known for its aromatic qualities. Rosemary is associated with remembrance.

Rosemary was traditionally regarded as a sacred herb and there are many legends surrounding it. One of them is that the Virgin Mary, on her flight into Egypt, threw her blue cloak over a rosemary bush to dry after washing it, and it honoured her by producing beautiful blue flowers. Another version of the legend is that she sheltered behind a rosemary bush by the roadside to escape her persecutors.

Rosemary also has a strong association with healing and the prevention of sickness. It was burned in ancient religious ceremonies to purify the air, and during the plague people sometimes carried little parcels of it, which they would sniff in the belief that it warded off the dreaded affliction. It is also said to keep away evil spirits, so for peace of mind gardeners should always find the space for one or two rosemary plants! The name Rosmarinus means "dew of the sea."

CULTIVATION

Rosemary is an asset to any garden, because besides being extremely useful it is a most attractive plant, with a fragrant aroma and pretty blue or white flowers. It is a hardy evergreen perennial that flowers throughout the year, but most prolifically in spring and autumn.

Conditions: Rosemary does well in most types of soil, although it prefers sandy, light soil that is well drained. It should be planted in a sunny position, whether indoors or out. Rosemary needs little water and thrives with the minimum of care.

Propagation: This is best done by taking a cutting with a small heel. It will root very quickly.

Containers: Rosemary grows well in huge pots placed on a very sunny patio. Make sure that the pot is adequate to the task as the plant grows rapidly and has a large root system.

Size: Grows to a height of between 60 and 180 cm.

Harvesting: Can be picked in small amounts all year round. Gather the main leaf crop before the plant flowers.

Dos and don'ts: Rosemary and sage make happy companions, so do plant them together. Rosemary repels carrot fly, but attracts bees and butterflies to the garden. It makes a superb hedge around the herb garden and benefits from clipping.

USES
Domestic
☐ To make an insecticide: mix 5 ml of rosemary oil with 300 ml of beer and spray onto plants or any other areas plagued by insects. The dried herb can also be powdered and mixed with equal quantities of dried wormwood, and then sprinkled in cupboards, along skirting boards or between rows of vegetables.

☐ Rosemary is excellent in potpourri, and stems of the plant can be placed in cupboards to keep linen fresh and sweet-smelling.

☐ The rosemary branch can be used to make decorative wreaths or garlands.

☐ Scatter rosemary stems on a braai to keep insects away and to flavour the braaiing chops.

Cosmetic
☐ Rosemary serves as the base for an effective hair lotion and rinse. It checks falling hair, stimulates and revitalises the hair, and treats eczema of the scalp. Cover a pot of rosemary sprigs in water, boil for 30 minutes, cool and strain. Massage into the scalp. The mixture can also be added to the final rinse water after shampooing. Keep any excess in the fridge to comb through the hair and massage into the scalp daily.

☐ To remove freckles and wrinkles, boil 50 g flowering rosemary tips in half a litre of white wine for two minutes. Leave for one hour to infuse. Strain and apply to the face with cotton wool every morning and evening.

Medicinal
☐ Rosemary has long been used to treat blood pressure abnormalities (it has the remarkable ability to level both

high and low blood pressure), headaches and heart ailments. It is increasingly being employed in the treatment of migraine, jaundice, fainting fits, vertigo, cirrhosis of the liver, gallstones, rheumatism and obesity.

□ Rosemary tea relieves physical and mental strain and provides an ideal tonic for convalescents. Make it by infusing a quarter cup of fresh flowering rosemary tips in a cup of boiling water. Leave for 5 minutes, strain and sweeten with honey if liked. Take morning and evening for no more than four days at a time. For liver complaints one tablespoon should be taken before each meal. This is also an effective way of easing indigestion.

□ When steeped in warmed wine rosemary imparts a delicious flavour. Rosemary in wine is also good for soothing sore throats, stuffy noses, winter chills and colds, and it has the added benefit of relieving digestion. Add 200 g of fresh rosemary leaves or 60 g dried leaves to a litre of red wine. Leave to infuse for 15 days, shaking occasionally. Strain and sweeten if desired. Take after meals, 1 tablespoon at a time. Or simply steep a piece of rosemary in the wine, warm it and add a piece of cinnamon and some sugar. Drink after 10 minutes.

□ The elixir made famous by the Queen of Hungary at the end of the 14th century, known as "Queen of Hungary water" is based on rosemary. A modern version can be made as follows:
Macerate 600 g of rosemary flowers and the flowering tips of rosemary with 900 ml ethyl alcohol (obtainable from a chemist) in a jar, then expose the jar, which must be well stoppered, to the sun for at least one month, shaking frequently. Finally strain and press through a fine cloth.

The Queen reported that she drank a dram of this powerful concoction once a week, and washed her face and gouty limbs with it. It cured her of gout and other infirmities, and she became so beautiful that even though she was 72 years old the King of Poland, on seeing her, proposed marriage!

Culinary

□ Rosemary leaf is a delicious flavouring for lamb, as well as bean and tomato dishes. It has a very strong flavour, though, and should always be used sparingly. Try a dash on baked potatoes and in herb butter.

□ Rosemary flowers, stripped of the tough calyx, can be used fresh in salads, fruit salads and drinks.

□ Rosemary leaves can be used to flavour wine. See section on medicinal uses.

□ Use the twigs, stripped of their leaves, for kebab skewers or for braaiing onions and green peppers. They impart a tantalising flavour to the food.

Creeping rosemary (R. officinalis prostratus)

Rosemary buttermilk rusks

500 g butter
6 cups wholewheat or brown bread flour
6 cups cakeflour
8 teaspoons baking powder
1–1½ cups sugar
2 cups coconut
pinch salt
6 tablespoons finely chopped fresh rosemary
little powdered nutmeg
3 eggs beaten with 1 litre buttermilk

Rub butter into flour. Add all the ingredients, the beaten eggs and buttermilk last, to form a stiff dough. Roll into balls about the size of golf balls and pack into well greased tins. Sprinkle with a little nutmeg, and bake for 1 hour at 375 °F/180 °C or until done.

When cool remove from the tins, breaking apart gently. Place on the oven rack or on a cake cooler in a 200 °F/100 °C oven overnight to dry out. Keep the oven door slightly ajar. When dry and cool, pack into tins.

YIELDS APPROX. 5 DOZ.

RUE/WYNRUIT
Ruta graveolens
Family: Rutaceae

The word "rue" means "sorrow" or "pity"' or "repent," and the leaves were once added to holy water used to bless sinners. Certain oriental cultures believe that rue will protect the household against evil influences. The plant should be handled with care as at certain times of year, particularly hot periods, it can cause a skin rash. This can be soothed by liberal applications of the juice and pulp of bulbinella (Bulbine frutescens). Rue has literally dozens of medicinal uses, from drawing abscesses and boils to relieving toothache, and was once found in almost every garden. The shape of rue leaves inspired the club design in the suit of playing cards.

CULTIVATION
Rue is a perennial plant that makes an attractive low hedge if kept clipped.

Conditions: Rue is not fussy about soil but prefers a slightly alkaline one. It does not like very damp soil and needs full sun.

Propagation: By seeds or cuttings. Cuttings may be taken at any time of year. Choose small, strong side shoots and press them into wet sand. Keep them moist until well rooted. Seed germinates if really fresh, but germination tends to be sporadic. Plant out 50 to 60 cm apart in a well-prepared bed. The roots go deep so make sure the holes go down far enough.

Size: Up to 1,5 m in height and width.

Harvesting: Trim the plants back from time to time; keep the trimmed pieces to use fresh, or dry them to use as an insecticide. Collect the seeds and pick young leaves just before the flowers open.

Dos and don'ts: Don't plant rue near basil as one or the other will die. Do locate it near peach trees or tomatoes to deter fruit flies and beetles. Do plant rue near roses to deter aphids, and edge vegetable gardens with it.

USES
Domestic
☐ Bags of fresh rue hung up in the house will drive flies and mosquitoes away. Dried rue twigs can also be sprinkled around plants to repel ants and other insects, and pushed down antholes. It will even keep worms away from strawberries – tuck under the straw and sprinkle over the plants. Keep a few rue twigs in the dog's kennel to deter fleas.
☐ The roots of rue produce a beautiful red dye.
☐ Rue leaves look good in insect repelling posies and small flower arrangements. Be careful not to touch it too much, though, as the smell is very powerful!

Cosmetic
☐ An infusion of rue leaves can be used as an eye bath. Make it by pouring 4 cups of boiling water over 1 tablespoon of fresh leaves. Draw for five minutes, then strain and cool.

Medicinal
☐ A lotion made with rue serves as an excellent drawing poultice for abscesses and boils.
☐ A rue decoction may be taken to relieve tiredness and anxiety. It is very strong, though, so dosages should be small. Five ml of chopped leaves added to 500 ml boiling water and left for 20 minutes is about the right concentration. The mixture should be strained and a small wineglassful taken twice daily for menstrual pain, heart palpitations, epilepsy, fevers, colic, worms, upset stomach, ringworm, and convulsions in children. It was once even used for snakebite! Applied externally the same mixture can be used for skin parasites, lice and eye ailments. It is advisable to consult your doctor first.
☐ In South Africa the rue decoction is used to treat typhoid fever and scarlet fever. The juice from the leaf was also once used to treat epilepsy and convulsions in children. Bunches of rue leaves tied up in a muslin bag and added to bathwater will help prevent convulsions.
☐ Apply a bruised rue leaf to relieve toothache. This is a favourite toothache remedy among the black peoples of southern Africa.

Culinary
☐ A very few rue leaves can be added to lovage and mint as a marinade for game birds.
☐ The leaves are bitter but in very small quantities add interesting flavour to fairly bland foods like cream cheese, eggs and fish.

SALAD BURNET/PIMPERNEL
Sanguisorba officinalis
Family: Rosaceae

This herb has a legendary ability to heal wounds. The story goes that many centuries ago, after a bloody battle King Chaba of Hungary used it to heal the wounds of 15 000 of his soldiers! Besides this property it has other medicinal uses and is a versatile culinary herb. It is native to Europe and the British Isles, where it is a particularly useful culinary plant as it withstands snow and can therefore be enjoyed all year round in its fresh green state.

CULTIVATION
Salad burnet is a hardy herbaceous perennial plant with attractive green, fern-like leaves and tiny green and yellowish spherical flowers.

Conditions: Salad burnet grows in an average soil, but likes moisture. It will do best in a sunny position.

Propagation: By seeds only. Seeds sown in moist sand germinate readily and once it is in the garden it seeds itself so prolifically that you will have to do nothing to encourage it. It can be separated as it becomes untidy if not controlled. If it is being used as a border edging plant it is advisable however to use new seedlings every season, as it stays neater this way.

Size: Grows to a height of 20-45 cm.

Harvesting: Cut flower heads back to encourage new leaf growth. Remove older leaves but use them fresh as it does not keep its flavour when dried or frozen. Remove fresh young leaves for use in salads.

Dos and don'ts: Salad burnet makes an ideal edging plant for your herb garden, and does particularly well near lettuce and marigolds. If interplanted with peas it seems to enhance their growth.

USES
Domestic
☐ The very attractive, fernlike leaves can be pressed into the sides of slightly melted candles for decoration, or used in posies. The flowers dry beautifully and are most suitable for dried flower arrangements and in pot-pourris.

Cosmetic
☐ A salad burnet infusion relieves sunburn and troubled skin, and soothes chilblains. Boil 2 cups of salad burnet leaves in 2 *l* of water for 10 minutes. Cool and strain. Use as a lotion.

Medicinal
☐ Besides its legendary wound-healing properties salad burnet has the effect of cooling the blood, and soothing sunburn and skin ailments. Pour 250 ml boiling water onto 8 mature leaf sprays, stand for 5 minutes and drink 125 ml morning and night. It also relieves haemorrhoids when used as a lotion, and diarrhoea when taken as a tea.

☐ Salad burnet leaves can be chewed after a heavy meal to aid digestion.

Culinary
☐ Salad burnet has a pleasant cucumber-like flavour and as its name suggests is excellent in salads. It can also be mixed into salad dressings or cream cheeses, but use young leaves only as the leaves become more stringy with age.

☐ Salad burnet can be used to make a delicious vinegar. Place a handful of leaves into a bottle of good quality white vinegar (or cider vinegar if you want to use it for coughs and sore throats). Place in the sun for 10 days, replacing the herb with fresh leaves at least three times. Strain and pour into fresh bottles, and decorate with a leaf spray or two.

☐ Add salad burnet leaves to soups and stews in the early stages of cooking.

☐ Salad burnet combines well with other herbs, especially rosemary and tarragon. A delicious fish sauce can be made with equal quantities of chopped burnet and tarragon or mint, added to 110 g melted butter and simmered for ten minutes.

☐ Add salad burnet leaves to summer drinks and punches.

SAGE/SALIE
Salvia officinalis
Family: Labiatae

The scientific name of this prince among herbs is derived from the Latin word "salvere" which means to enjoy good health, to cure or to save. Its name reflects the benevolent qualities of the herb. The Romans regarded it as sacred, and believed that it had to be gathered according to a prescribed ritual. Besides having powerful healing properties it is a prominent culinary herb, often used on its own. It is used in both sweet and savoury dishes, and has the property of helping in the digestion of fatty acids. Sage is also extremely aromatic and an absolutely essential component of the herb garden. There are several other varieties of sage, with varying strengths of flavour, including S. sclarea (clary), S. purpurescens (purple sage), S. variegata (golden sage) and S. elegans (pineapple sage).

CULTIVATION
Sage is a hardy perennial

Conditions: Sage likes full sun and a poor, dry, well-drained soil. Clary prefers partial shade, or shade in the afternoon.

Propagation: By cuttings or seed (if fresh). Cuttings can be taken at any time of the year from garden sage and pineapple sage, excepting during the coldest months, and new plants should be kept growing continuously to replace those that die. Fresh seed germinates well. Clary is quite a tall variety that can be grown in the back of the bed. Pineapple sage is also quite tall, reaching 90 cm if planted in suitable soil, and has pretty bright red edible flowers.

Containers: If the seedlings are transplanted when just big enough to handle they make excellent pot plants. They should be planted in a sandy soil mixture and the pots should be well drained. Stand sage plants in full sun, for example on a balcony or patio, and water once a week and twice in very hot weather.

Size: Grows to a height of 30–90 cm depending on species.

Harvesting: Pick the leaves just before the flowers come out.

Dos and don'ts: Do grow sage near rosemary as they stimulate one another. Sage leaves make an excellent fertiliser when mixed with wood-ash and manure, so save old leaves if plants die, and gather fallen leaves under the bushes. Sage repels cabbage moths, so plant near cabbages if you have any. Sage does not like having water sprayed on its leaves, or waterlogged soil. Cut back the flowering spikes after they fade and keep the bushes trimmed.

USES
Domestic
☐ The sage leaf looks very attractive in wreaths.

☐ The flowers of clary (*S. sclarea*) are excellent in flower arrangements. Pineapple sage has a lovely red flower that makes an attractive addition to potpourris.

☐ Put dried sage leaves among linen to discourage insects.

☐ Burn leaves on embers or boil in water to disinfect a room. Sage smoke deodorises unpleasant smells.

☐ All sages have insect-repelling properties, so grow a row to add to insect sprays.

Cosmetic
☐ Sage leaves can be used in facial steams and to produce an astringent cleansing lotion.

☐ Use a rinse made from sage leaves to condition and darken grey hair.

☐ Rub sage leaves on teeth to whiten, and add to mouthwash.

☐ A sage brew makes a good deodorising wash for underarms and feet. Make it by boiling 2 cups of sprigs in 2 *l* of water for 20 minutes, then cooling.

Medicinal
☐ The leaf is a digestive aid with antiseptic and antifungal properties. A sage sandwich or a sage tea after a meal aids digestion.

☐ Sage tea is also a nerve tonic and used in the treatment of coughs and colds, and even irregular menstruation. It also helps memory retention. Make the tea by pouring a cup of boiling water over a quarter cup of fresh sage leaves. Allow to stand for 5 minutes then strain. Add a little honey if desired.

Culinary

☐ The flower may be scattered in salads or infused to make a tea.

☐ The leaf is mixed with onion to make poultry stuffing, and in the cooking of all rich, fatty meats. It is also excellent blended into cheeses.

☐ The leaves of clary sage are delicious fried in batter and eaten with lamb dishes.

☐ Sage leaf can be dried for culinary purposes by hanging it in bunches or laying it on a rack in the shade. When dry it can be crumbled and stored in glass bottles for winter use. Fresh sage tastes much nicer than dried, however.

☐ *Salvia officinalis icterina*, a golden, variegated sage, has a milder flavour than common sage. It garnishes and flavours chicken, fish and egg dishes excellently.

Pineapple sage
(S. elegans)

Sage and onion stuffing

I find this a particularly pleasing stuffing for duck and turkey, and it turns an ordinary roast chicken into a gala dish. It is very quick and easy to make, and can be sprinkled over the top of a chicken casserole or braai for extra taste, as one would sprinkle breadcrumbs.

  Substitute cream for the yoghurt, sprinkle over fish and bake uncovered for 10 minutes to brown and crisp. Or serve over grilled chicken or sausage.

1 cup plain yoghurt
1–2 cups brown breadcrumbs, depending on the preferred consistency
¹/₂ cup chopped sage
1 cup chopped onion
salt and pepper
cardamom or allspice to taste
¹/₂–1 tablespoon debittered brewers yeast
juice of 1 lemon

Optional

¹/₂ cup sunflower seeds
or ¹/₂ cup mung bean sprouts
or ¹/₂ cup alfalfa (lucerne) sprouts
or ¹/₂ cup buckwheat greens

Mix all the ingredients together and stuff the bird, or add a little wheat germ and use it as a topping for casseroles and grills.

SOAPWORT/SEEPKRUID
Saponaria officinalis
Family: Caryophyllaceae

This is an extremely attractive herb with the added advantage of being useful, and it grows almost everywhere. As its name suggests, it yields a soapy sap (saponin) which can be used to clean delicate and expensive fabrics. The pink blooms are most fragrant, particularly in the hot weather and at night. The herb has been used in the Middle East for a long time both for cleaning and to treat skin problems. The herb is also known as Bouncing Bet, Australian phlox and Fuller's herb.

CULTIVATION
Soapwort is a hardy herbaceous perennial but is extremely invasive, so take the trouble to contain it.
Conditions: Soapwort withstands any soil, will flower only in full sun, and suckers everywhere.
Propagation: By division or runners. Prepare a bed that has been lined with a 45-cm strip of heavy duty plastic, add a few spadefuls of compost (2 spades to one square metre of soil), loosen well and plant root runners or pieces of root. Water well at first; thereafter give a weekly watering. Add an annual dressing of compost. Cut back flowering heads.
Size: Grows to a height of 15-40 cm.
Harvesting: The flowers, leaves, stems and roots can be picked as required. The roots are richest in saponin. The flowers and leaves may be dried, while the roots may be sliced up and dried in the sun, but as it is perennial it is best used fresh all year round.

Dos and don'ts: As the roots of soapwort are invasive, it is a good idea to plant it in an open-ended shallow drum or open pipe sunk into the ground to contain the roots.

USES
Domestic
☐ The leaf, stem and root may be covered in rainwater or distilled water and boiled for 30 minutes; the soapy liquid that is produced can be used to wash delicate old fabrics such as tapestries.
☐ Soapwort was used as a water softener in Roman times.
☐ The flowers may be used to perfume rooms in the house.
☐ Dried soapwort flowers may be used in potpourri.

Cosmetic
☐ The leaf, stem and root may be boiled in water to produce a wash suitable for hair and delicate skin. Pick enough to fill a big pot – cover with water and simmer for 20 minutes. Keep covered all the time, and cool until pleasantly warm. Be careful not to get it in the eyes. It will rebuild hair that is dry and damaged by anaesthesia, and will soothe and soften the skin.

Medicinal
☐ A decoction made from the root, leaves and stem can be used to treat psoriasis and acne. The root is poisonous, though, and should not be taken internally. Boil 2 cups of leaves, stems and root in a litre of water for 15 minutes. Strain, cool and use as a lotion.
☐ The soapy bubbles made by rubbing the leaves and stems together vigorously are excellent if smeared on eczema areas and allowed to dry.

Culinary
☐ Scatter the flower petals on salads and fruit salads – the flower is quite edible but can be rather soapy if chewed.

SORREL/SURING

Rumex acetosa
Family: Polygonaceae

Sorrel is a general name given to several indigenous species and some introduced species. The indigenous yellow or wood sorrel, Oxalis pes-caprae (wilde, geel-of klawersuring) is the one generally used in South African cooking, and has yellow flowers and triangular, lobed leaves. It dies down in midsummer.

The real large-leafed European sorrel (R. acetosa) is a very useful cooking herb that also has medicinal properties. It should not be eaten by those suffering from arthritis, gout, rheumatism or hyperacidity, because of its high acid content. Sorrel is also known as "sour dock," for this reason (it is related to dock). It should also not be consumed by old people or children. R. acetosa is widely used in European cuisine. It was used in ancient Greece, Rome and Egypt, often as an antidote for overeating or too much drinking. It is best used fresh or cooked as little as possible, cut with a stainless steel knife and prepared in stainless steel or unchipped enamel pots, as its acidity is so high it reacts with iron and turns everything black and metallic tasting.

CULTIVATION

Conditions: Sorrel likes a fairly rich, moist soil and a sunny position, though it is happy to be in the shade in the afternoon.

Propagation: From seeds or by division. If propagating from seed, sow as early in spring as you can as the plant needs as long a growing season as possible. Plant seedlings out 45 to 60 cm apart. Cut back flowering stems to keep the plant perennial. Well-established plants can be divided and the shoots successfully replanted.

Containers: The indigenous sorrel *Oxalis pes-caprae* can be grown in pots in the sun. The large-leafed sorrel can be grown in a large tub in the sun.

Size: Up to 60 cm in height.

Harvesting: Leaves for cooking should be gathered when young.

Dos and don'ts: Do use *O. pes-caprae* as an edging plant; its yellow flowers make a lovely show in spring. Do plant the large sorrel near marigolds and rue to keep insects away from it. Use old leaves in the compost, as they are excellent compost decomposers.

USES

Domestic
☐ The leaf of *R. acetosa* can be used to bleach rust and ink stains from linen, silver and wicker. Crush and pound the leaves and spread onto the area, leaving for 20 minutes. Wash off with mild detergent.

Cosmetic
☐ Sorrel leaves are effective in combating acne and skin disorders if applied as a poultice. The Tswana people apply indigenous sorrels to sores and pimples.

Medicinal
☐ Sorrel is used by some black tribes to treat abscesses.
☐ The root has a diuretic and tonic effect.
☐ The leaf of *R. acetosa* may be infused as a tea to treat kidney and liver ailments, but large doses may cause kidney damage. The standard brew is a cup of boiling water poured over a quarter cup of fresh chopped leaves. Stand for 5 minutes, strain and take one cup daily for no more than three days.
☐ Sorrel has a high oxalic content and was once much prized in the treatment of scurvy. The corms or "bulbs" of the indigenous varieties were taken on board ships in the early days of the Cape settlement to keep the sailors free of this dread disease.

Culinary
☐ Fresh, young sorrel leaves are delicious in salads, omelettes and scrambled eggs.
☐ Cook a few leaves with spinach and cabbage.
☐ The leaves can be cooked as a vegetable, but change the water during cooking to reduce acidity.
☐ Sorrel soup, made with chicken stock, lovage, celery and onions with a sorrel base, is a gourmet's treat.
☐ Sorrel combines well with herbs like thyme, marjoram, chives, onions and lovage.
☐ The indigenous variety of sorrel is used in traditional and Cape Malay cooking; it is especially delicious in waterblommetjiebredie.

SOUR FIG/HOTNOTSVY OF SUURVY
Carpobrotus edulis
Family: Mesembryanthemaceae

This indigenous low-growing plant was first exploited by the indigenous peoples of the Cape for its medicinal properties. It has distinctive three-angled succulent leaves containing an antiseptic, astringent juice that can be used internally and externally for a number of complaints. The fruit or "fig" is also used for medicinal purposes, and made into delicious jams and preserves that are a true Cape delicacy. Dried sour figs are generally available at produce markets in the Cape and Natal. There are several varieties of sour fig, some with yellow flowers and others with bright magenta ones. Like the pelargoniums, the sour fig was taken to Europe quite early on in the history of the Cape, and can now be seen growing in several places including the shores of the Mediterranean and the south coast of England.

CULTIVATION
Sour fig is a perennial that thrives on poor, sandy soil (it is often found on dunes) and needs very little water. To propagate just stick a runner or piece of stem into the ground (70 to 100 cm apart) and keep wet for a few days. Cut back the plant if it gets too invasive.

USES
Domestic
☐ The leaf juice can be applied to infected tick and flea bites on dogs to stop them scratching. Pat onto the afflicted parts 3 times a day.

Cosmetic
☐ The leaf juice can be dabbed onto acne spots. A cup of crushed leaves, covered by a litre of boiling water and strained when cool, can be used as an astringent lotion for oily, spotty skins.

Medicinal
☐ Chew a leaf tip if you have a sore throat. The juice from the leaves soothes mouth infections, sore throats and indigestion. An old Boer recipe for a throat gargle consists of equal parts of vinegar, honey and sour fig leaf juice. It is also a traditional remedy for diarrhoea and dysentery. The juice can also soothe and heal burns. Keep some of the dried fruit at hand to make gargles and mouthwashes when the fresh plant is unavailable. Boil up 10 dried figs in 4 cups of water. The spring honey from the flowers also has a soothing effect on sore throats when mixed in hot water and sipped.
☐ The leaf juice can be applied to the skin to soothe ringworm, infantile eczema and sunburn.
☐ One of the best-known uses of sour fig leaves is as an antidote for bluebottle stings – handy as it is often found growing on dunes near the beach. Rub the afflicted area frequently with the juice from the leaves.
☐ The Khoi (Hottentot) women used to drink an infusion made from the fruit to ensure an easy birth. The newborn infant was also smeared with the juice to make it nimble and strong.

Culinary
☐ The ripe fruits ("figs") can be eaten fresh or dried and made into a delicious jam.

SOUTHERNWOOD/AWERUIT
Artemisia abrotanum
Family: Compositae

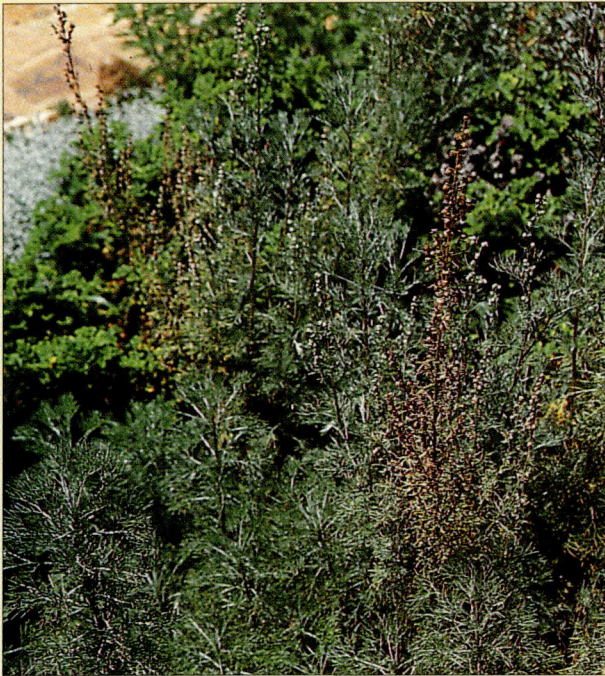

Southernwood is one of the Artemesia species, named after Artemisia, the sister and wife of the Persian King Mausolus, who was a renowned botanist. The genus includes 200 plants, most of them aromatic. Southernwood has a pungent lemony scent. Other members of the genus include wormwood and mugwort. Southernwood is woody stemmed, with distinctive feathery leaves that make it a very decorative plant. In the olden days it was spread on floors to sweeten the air and keep rooms free of insects. The leaves were added to a face cream that was believed to encourage the growth of a young man's beard — hence its other name, "Lad's love."

CULTIVATION
Southernwood is a bushy perennial.

Conditions: Southernwood is unfussy about soil but likes it dry. It thrives in full sun.

Propagation: Can be by division or cuttings. Where its branches touch the ground it roots easily. A quick way to make rooted cuttings is to press a hoop of wire over a low-growing branch so that it touches the earth, and let it send down roots. In a week or two the stem can be cut from the main plant, left briefly to harden and strengthen, and then moved to its new site. Cuttings can be taken at any time of the year and root easily in wet sand.

Plant them out 90 cm apart as the bushes grow as wide as they are tall.

Size: Southernwood grows to between 60 cm and 1,2 m.

Harvesting: Cut back at the end of the growing season, around July, and shape the bushes, but trim throughout the year. Keep all cut branches for use as insect repellents and in potpourris.

Dos and don'ts: Do plant southernwood as a low hedge, near cabbages if you have them as it protects them from aphids and other insects. If it is planted near fruit trees it will repel fruit fly and night-feeding fruit moths. It benefits from constant pruning and can be easily shaped into topiaries and hedges.

USES
Domestic
☐ The leaves of southernwood are very effective in repelling insects. Sprays can be placed in and behind books to repel fish moths.

☐ Southernwood is a very effective addition to potpourris.

☐ Stripped branches placed on a braai will keep insects away, and on interior fires will clear the air of cooking smells.

☐ Those gardeners who are keen on home-made "green" products might like to try the following general spray for aphids and other small pests. Combine equal quantities of southernwood, khakibos, wormwood, tansy, wilde als and, if you live at the sea, any type of seaweed. Chop and steep in enough boiling water to cover, stand overnight and strain the next morning. Add a cup of soap powder to a 5-litre bucket of the brewed mixture, as well as half a cup of mineral turpentine and four cups of sifted ash made from burned twigs, leaves and newspapers. The ash acts as a foliar feed. Splash or spray this brew onto the plants once a week to clear them of insects. Repeat after rain.

☐ To combat ants, dried, powdered southernwood can be sprinkled around ant holes, or push a fresh twig down the hole.

Cosmetic
☐ A light tea of southernwood can be used as a final rinse for greasy hair and, if combed through the hair, will stimulate growth. Make it by pouring 2 *l* of boiling water over a cup of fresh southernwood leaves, leave to stand until lukewarm then strain.

Medicinal
☐ The leaf of southernwood can be infused in a tea to make a tonic. The standard brew is a quarter cup of fresh leaves to one cup of boiling water. Stand five minutes then strain. Take 1 tablespoon twice daily to help build resistance to infections, or after a long illness. The same tea is an excellent lotion for rashes, scratches and grazes.

SUNFLOWER/SONNEBLOM
Helianthus annuus
Family: Compositae

The giant sunflower, so familiar in the rural South African landscape, is indigenous to Central and South America. It was cultivated there by the American Indians as far back as 3 000 years ago. The sunflower motif had great prominence in the Aztec religion. The plant was brought to Europe by the Spanish conquistadors. It was introduced to South Africa as a food crop for livestock and poultry. Few crops are as aesthetically appealing as the sunflower. The kernels of the sunflower seed, borne in the centre of the enormous yellow-fringed flowers, are extremely nutritious, comprising 25 percent protein and containing many vitamins and minerals. The seeds are an important source of cooking oil and also used in the manufacture of margarine.

CULTIVATION
Propagation: Prepare the soil by digging deeply, then add compost and water well. Make furrows, into which you sow the seed, 40 cm apart, and press in no more than 2 cm deep. Cover with a light mulch of leaves and keep moist until the seeds germinate. Thereafter water twice weekly.
Size: Sunflowers can grow to a height of 1,5 to 2 m.
Harvesting: Pick off the side buds for the pot when they reach 2 to 4 cm in diameter. Allow the main flower to dry completely before reaping.
Dos and don'ts: Sunflowers and potatoes stunt one another's growth. Cucumber grows well near sunflowers, however. You will find that the bees literally make a "beeline" for the sunflowers because of their nectar and pollen, and the birds will love the seeds. Plant sunflowers as a screen – they make a spectacular annual "hedge" that you will enjoy for months.

USES
Domestic
☐ Sunflowers draw large quantities of potash from the soil and when the dried stalks are burned the ash makes a good fertiliser.
☐ The dried heads may be cut off in autumn and given to poultry as a special treat.
☐ Smaller flower heads, if picked when ripe and just starting to dry, can be hung upside down, dried, and used in dry flower arrangements.
☐ The yellow petals can be used to make a yellow dye.
☐ An infusion of the young sunflower will kill flies. Pour boiling water over the chopped flowers until they are covered, steep overnight and then strain. Use the brew to spray or wipe down windows and window sills.
☐ The pith from the stem is one of the lightest substances known and is used to make paper.

Cosmetic
☐ Sunflower seeds contain vitamin F and other substances that nourish the skin.

Medicinal
☐ Hulled sunflower seeds are said to be diuretic and expectorant. A handful can be eaten once or twice a day or the unhulled seed can be boiled for 20 minutes and taken as a tea. Add 2 tablespoons of unshelled seeds to 2 cups of water then simmer for 20 minutes. Cool and strain. Take half a cup twice a day.
☐ Sunflower leaves have been used as a remedy for malaria, and in Italy parts of the plant are used as a diuretic, febrifuge and stimulant.

Culinary
☐ Sunflower seeds are delicious raw or roasted in home-made breakfast cereals, such as muesli.
☐ The lesser buds growing off the main stem can be cooked and eaten like artichokes, with butter and vinegar.
☐ To make an energy-giving sweet for hikers and runners, grind hulled sunflower seeds with equal quantities of sesame seeds and mix to a stiff dough with honey. Pinch off small balls and roll them in coconut.

ST JOHN'S WORT/KERRIEBOS

Hypericum perforatum
Family: Guttiferae

This is a fragrant herb with pale green leaves and lemon-scented yellow flowers. It is a garden plant in South Africa, but in England it is found growing wild in the countryside. It has recently been found growing wild as a weed in the Cape province. The poppy-shaped flowers when steeped in olive oil yield the famous "oil of St John's wort," which was used as far back as the Crusades. The oil extracted from the leaves is used extensively in the USA to treat cuts and bruises. It is known there as Turkey red oil. The whole plant has healing properties, and is also known as "touch and heal." It was once believed to protect the home from harm and loss, and used extensively for magic charms. Putting bunches of the flowers in your house was said to be a way of attracting fairies! There are 500 varieties of Hypericum, not all of which can be used medicinally.

CULTIVATION

St John's wort is a hardy perennial shrub that thrives on little attention. It grows into a somewhat untidy shape.
Conditions: The plant likes sun or light shade and will grow in most soils.
Propagation: Take cuttings from runners at the base of the plant (in spring or summer), or grow from seed. Press cuttings into wet sand. Try to pull off twigs with a "heel" attached and keep protected by making a plastic greenhouse tent over the box. Keep well watered until the cuttings have rooted. Transplant into bags and keep protected and damp until well established. Harden off by increasing the time they are exposed to the sun each day and plant out 90 cm apart.
Size: 15 cm to 1,8 m high.
Harvesting: Pick flowers at any time of the year.
Dos and don'ts: The plants need full sun. Prune them twice yearly for tidiness.

USES
Domestic
The flowers can be used to make a yellow dye.

Cosmetic
Crushed petals can be added to rain water and applied to thread veins on the face, or mashed into aqueous cream and applied to bruises for soothing relief.

Medicinal
☐ The entire plant is antibiotic, and this antibiotic has been patented overseas as a possible food preservative.
☐ The infused flower oil helps heal bruises, wounds, ulcers, sunburn, etc. Make an infusion by adding 5 flowers to 250 ml boiling water, let it stand for five minutes and strain. This can also be taken as a tea.
☐ In Europe the plant is used to treat dysentery, rabies and sciatica, among other ailments, and applied to wounds.
☐ The flowers can be infused to make a sedative tea to treat anaemia, rheumatism, bad nerves and headaches. The tea can be made as for the infusion above, but take only 37,5 ml three times a day. Some people consider it unsafe, however, so discuss it with your doctor.

TANSY/WURMKRUID
Tanacetum vulgare
Family: Compositae

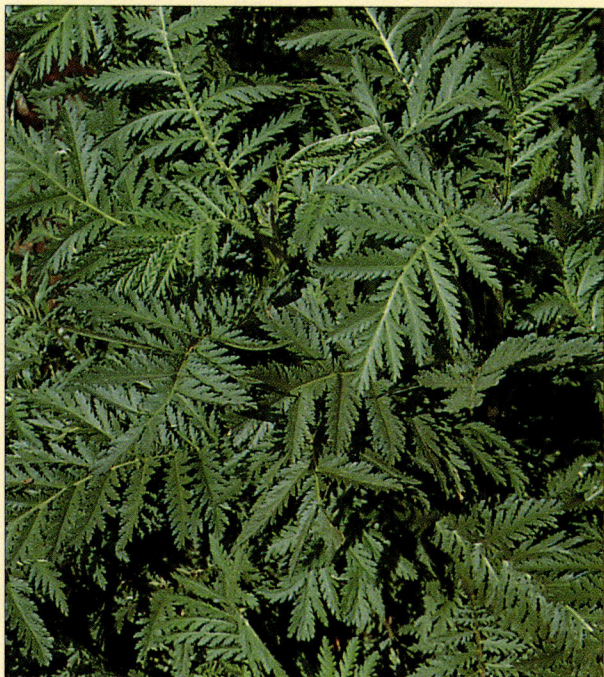

Tansy is well known for its brilliant yellow dye, once used to colour cakes and confectionery. It is rich in minerals and has many medicinal uses. The name is believed to derive from the Greek word "athanatos," meaning "immortality." It was so called because it was believed to arrest decay. It is strongly antiseptic and was once used to preserve corpses. It was an important strewing herb and also used as a flavouring, being valued for its rich, gingery taste, particularly in tansy pudding, a rich custard-like dish. It is native to Europe and Asia, but grows freely, even as a weed, in many countries.

CULTIVATION
Tansy is an easy plant to grow. It tends to spread and dies back in winter.

Conditions: Not fussy about soil but likes a sunny exposure.

Propagation: By division or seeds. The rooted side shoots can be removed in spring and planted in new ground 60 cm apart. Both *T. vulgare* and *T. crispum*, the curly tansy or sun fern much used by florists, grow easily from seed and if conditions are right both seed themselves or send out runners.

Size: Grows up to 90 cm, including its flowering head.

Harvesting: Cut off the aromatic leaves repeatedly for drying or fresh use. They are also benefical when added to compost, as they concentrate potassium.

Dos and don'ts: Do plant tansy between peach trees to keep fruitfly and fruit moths away.

USES
Domestic
☐ The tall flowering head is a beautiful florist's bloom. It retains its bright colour when dried and is ideal for dried winter arrangements and potpourris.

☐ Tansy has a very strong smell and when dried can be combined with other pungent herbs to make a natural insecticide for sprinkling in insect-infested areas. If rubbed into a dog's coat it will keep fleas away.

☐ Tansy flowers can be boiled to produce a lovely yellow dye, and the leaf boiled to produce a yellowy green woollen dye.

☐ Hang tansy leaves up in the house to keep flies away.

☐ Meat can be wrapped in tansy leaves to keep it fresh.

Cosmetic
☐ The flower and leaf may be added to baths and facial steams to revitalise mature and sallow skin in particular, but should be avoided if you have a sensitive skin.

Medicinal
☐ Tansy is good for fevers, kidney ailments, digestive complaints, jaundice and menstrual disorders. It is also an aid in reducing high blood pressure and strengthening the heart. The standard lotion is 5 ml chopped herb to 250 ml boiling water; stand for 5 minutes and strain. A dose of 12,5 ml should be taken three times a day before meals. Tansy is very strong and the recommended dose should not be exceeded. It should not be used during pregnancy. Remember to consult your doctor before using it!

☐ A tansy brew made as above can be used as a gargle to cure mouth infections; and in small doses for clearing worms in children. Give no more than 2 teaspoonfuls daily.

☐ Used externally tansy is excellent for varicose veins, swellings, bruises, earache, sties and eye inflammation. The same brew as above can be applied hot, by soaking a cotton cloth and holding the wrung cloth to the affected area.

Culinary
☐ Collect the flowers, then dry and powder them to make a useful colouring for cakes. One dessertspoon can be added to 450 g of flour.

☐ Tansy leaf may be stewed with rhubarb – but in very small amounts only.

☐ Rub a little of the leaf on meat before cooking to flavour.

☐ Tansy was traditionally used (very sparingly) to flavour sausages, meat pies and stuffings.

☐ It can be added as a flavouring in custards, rice puddings and milk sauces. It has the added benefit of soothing stomach complaints when used sparingly.

TARRAGON/DRAGON

Artemisia dracunculoides, A. dracunculus
Family: Compositae

Tarragon (A. dracunculoides)

The name "tarragon" derives from the Latin word for "dragon," which is also its Afrikaans name. This may be because it has a fiery taste or because its roots are serpent-like. It was also once believed to cure the bites of venomous creatures. Today tarragon is best known as a culinary herb. A. dracunculoides is also known as Russian tarragon. It is much hardier than the other variety, A. dracunculus or French tarragon, but has a coarser flavour. French tarragon can be distinguished from the Russian variety by its thicker, coarser leaves. French tarragon is an indispensable ingredient in French cuisine.

CULTIVATION

Tarragon is a perennial plant and dies down in the winter, sending up new growth in spring.

Conditions: Tarragon likes light, well-drained and moderately rich soil, sun or partial shade. All it needs is a yearly dressing of compost, one spadeful per plant, which should be dug in during the dormant period in winter. In autumn cut the plant back to 5 cm and cover with a layer of grass and leaves to protect the leaves from winter frost. As it tends to lose its flavour as it gets older, try to have some new cuttings ready at all times. One way of doing this is to dig up a clump, separate the side shoots from the mother plant, select the more robust suckers and replant them in the same place. Add a little compost and discard the mother plant. Water well until they establish themselves. Thereafter water once or twice a week, as the plants tend to wilt on very hot days.

Propagation: This can be done by root cutting or division. The plants die down in winter and send out new growth in spring. The plants should be separated or cuttings taken in August. A piece of rooted cutting, pressed into loosely dug soil and kept moist, will quickly establish and give no further trouble. Separate the clump every second or third year and cut and replant invading runners 60 cm apart.

Size: Tarragon grows up to a metre tall.

Harvesting: Leaves can be picked at any time, but the main crop is in late summer. If you want to remove whole branches, cut off at least two-thirds of the branch to permit regrowth.

Dos and don'ts: Tarragon will attract butterflies to your garden.

USES

Domestic
☐ Cut tarragon is excellent in compost making as it quickly breaks down tough leaves and stalks.

Cosmetic
☐ A crushed tarragon leaf pressed over a pimple helps to bring it to a head, and it was once used in antiseptic lotions for skin problems.

Medicinal
☐ If chewed, tarragon leaves will sweeten the breath and act as a soporific.
☐ The leaves are rich in vitamins and minerals.
☐ An infusion can be made as a tonic, appetite stimulant and aid to digestion. It was once used to combat scurvy. The standard brew is a cup of boiling water poured over a quarter cup of fresh leaves. Stand for 5 minutes and strain.
☐ The leaves of tarragon can be used to ease toothache if pressed into the painful tooth.

Culinary
☐ The tarragon leaf imparts a subtle, delicious flavour to food. Together with chervil and parsley it is used in *fines herbes*. It is used to make tarragon vinegar, bearnaise, tartar and hollandaise sauces. Tarragon vinegar can be made by filling a bottle of good white vinegar with several sprays of tarragon. Place it in the sun for 100 hours and during that period replace the tarragon sprays with fresh ones ten times. Strain, rebottle and add a spray of fresh tarragon for decoration.
☐ The leaves can be shredded and added to avocado fillings, mayonnaise, salad dressings, soups, omelettes, etc. Add to dishes just before serving.
☐ Tarragon makes a delicious herb butter for use on meats and vegetables.
☐ Add tarragon to chicken stuffing, preserves, pickles and mustards.

THYME/TIEMIE
Thymus species
Family: Labiatae

Thyme (T. vulgaris)

The various thyme species are grown for a variety of purposes: for ground cover, ornamental plants or as a culinary flavouring. The most common one is T. vulgaris, which grows as a woody-stemmed upright bush. T. serpyllum is also known as creeping thyme, and as its name suggests it makes a good ground cover and can be used to line a narrow path to create your own thyme walk. These were popular in the fifteenth, sixteenth and seventeenth centuries. Ladies would walk down the paths, which were just wide enough to accommodate their full skirts, and the skirts would brush the thyme border and release the aroma of thyme. Both T. vulgaris and T. serpyllum have medicinal properties. T. aureus or golden thyme, and T. argenteus, silver thyme, have wider leaf margins than the other varieties and a delicious lemony fragrance and flavour, as does lemon thyme (T. x citriodorus). Thyme is one of the most popular and universally used herbs, with a multitude of culinary and medicinal uses. It has been historically associated with happiness, courage and wellbeing. In fact the name is derived from the Greed word "thymon," meaning "courage." In the ancient world thyme was used as incense and burned to fumigate temples and other places. The thyme species are native to Europe and grow wild in the Mediterranean. The Egyptians and Etruscans used the herb for embalming, and in Greece thyme was used to anoint the body.

CULTIVATION
Thyme is a perennial plant.

Conditions: Thyme likes a sunny exposure and a dry, light soil that is well drained.

Propagation: By cuttings or from seeds. Plant seedlings or cuttings of *T. vulgaris* 30 cm apart and dig the bed deeply as the plants have long roots. Lightly compost the bed before planting out. *T. serpyllum* is easily propagated by cuttings and rooted pieces.

Containers: Thyme may be grown in pots, but needs full sun.

Size: Reaches 5 to 30 cm in height, depending on species.

Harvesting: Pick at any time of year; the plants benefit from constant picking.

Dos and don'ts: Thyme has an enlivening effect on neighbouring plants and is ideal as a border plant for the vegetable garden. It contains a fragrant oil, thymol, that repels aphids and moths so can be grown beneficially next to plants plagued by these insects. Do plant thyme if you want to attract bees to your garden.

USES
Domestic
☐ Thyme flowers and leaves make an attractive addition to posies.

☐ The leaves can be used to make a decoction suitable for use as a household disinfectant.

☐ If the essential oil of thyme is mixed with alcohol it can be used to protect paper and plants from mould.

☐ The thyme leaf and flowers can be used in potpourri.

Cosmetic
☐ A cup of *T. serpyllum* boiled in a litre of water for 15 minutes, cooled, strained and rubbed into the scalp daily will help stop hair loss. It can also be infused with rosemary to make an anti-dandruff hair rinse and to stimulate hair growth.

☐ A decoction of the thyme leaf stimulates skin circulation and can be used in baths and facial steams.

☐ The essential oil can be added to home-made toothpastes and mouthwashes as an antiseptic.

Medicinal
☐ Thyme is known for its antiseptic, digestive and antispasmodic properties. A brew of thyme, particularly the lemon-scented *T. x citriodorus*, will relieve coughs, colds and chills. To make it, take two thumb-length pieces of thyme and pour 250 ml of boiling water over them. Stand for five minutes, strain and add a teaspoonful or two of honey if liked. Drink before going to bed.

☐ A hot fomentation of *T. vulgaris* can be applied to boils and abscesses and brings on perspiration in fevers.

☐ *T. vulgaris* has been used as an antiseptic, carminative, digestive and enema, among many other medical uses.

☐ In the Western Cape a tincture of *T. serpyllum* is used

as a remedy for diarrhoea and abdominal cramps, as well as heart conditions. It is also used for whooping cough and respiratory ailments. In France it is used to treat skin conditions, and in Russia to relieve neuralgia and rheumatism.

Culinary

☐ Fresh *T. vulgaris* is used in many meat, cheese, egg and fish dishes. It can even be used on its own fried in batter to make a delicious thyme fritter. It makes a tasty and aromatic garnish for roasts and salad dressings, and fresh sprigs may be added to salads.

☐ Thyme has the ability to aid the digestion of fatty foods, and so makes a suitable addition to fatty meat roasts and other dishes high in fat.

☐ Thyme tastes particularly good when added to food cooked slowly in wine, including game.

☐ The lemon-flavoured thymes can be used to make delicious summer drinks, and added to sweet dishes like stewed fruits, custards and puddings.

☐ The Bedouin Arabs use thyme to make their delicious and well known condiment called Za'atar. Prepared from dried thyme, crushed coriander, sesame seeds and rock salt then pounded and mixed with olive oil, it is delicious on bread or used as a salad dressing.

☐ Thyme is used as an ingredient in bouquet garni. It combines well with milder herbs such as tarragon, watercress, chives, parsley, chervil, bay, dill, mint and so on, but because of its pungent taste it does not combine well with spices.

☐ Thyme makes an excellent herbal vinegar for use as a base for salad dressing.

Golden thyme (T. aureus)

Thyme and lemon sauce

2 tablespoons fresh thyme stripped off the stalks
1 teaspoon crushed coriander seeds
juice of 2 lemons
1 tablespoon honey

Crush the thyme and coriander and mix everything together. Shake the mixture up in a screw-top jar. Serve over fish, cheese, pasta or bean dishes.

Lemon thyme tea

1 cup boiling water
¼ cup fresh lemon thyme sprigs
1 piece cinnamon
juice of half a lemon
honey for sweetening

Pour boiling water over the lemon thyme and cinnamon, stand and strain. Sweeten with honey and add juice. Drink hot.

If you make a large quantity, calculate 2–3 thumb-length sprigs per person, and add more boiling water if it is too strong. Save any that is over for a delicious cool drink base. Just add lemon or orange juice and a little honey and decorate with mint sprigs. Serve in long glasses with ice.

SERVES 1

VIOLET/VIOOLTJIE
Viola odorata
Family: Violaceae

The violet is not usually regarded as a herb, although it has several culinary and medicinal applications. It is native to Britain and temperate Europe, but it now grows well in many parts of the world. The flowers have a beautiful colour and scent and are an asset to any garden. The violet has long been cultivated commercially for its perfume. The Greeks considered violet, also called sweet violet, to be a symbol of fertility, while the Romans made wine from it. It reached the height of its popularity as a scent in Victorian times, and is now coming back into favour.

CULTIVATION
Violet is a prolific perennial plant which is low growing and makes a good ground cover.

Conditions: Violet is shade-loving but will tolerate sun. It prefers a moist, fairly rich soil.

Propagation: By division. After dividing prepare a bed by digging in compost and a little old manure and water well. Space violet clumps about 30 cm apart. Keep shaded for the first few days.

Size: Grows to about 15 cm in height.

Harvesting: Pick leaves all year round and flowers soon after opening. The more flowers you pick, the more they bloom.

Dos and don'ts: Do plant violets if you want to attract butterflies to your garden. They make excellent edgings, are undemanding and always look good.

USES
Domestic
☐ Violets are a lovely addition to posies and bouquets.
☐ Use the flowers in potpourri.

Cosmetic
☐ Add violet leaves to steam for a facial.
☐ The flower may be decocted to use as an eyebath or mouthwash.
☐ Crushed violet leaves and flowers in almond oil soften callused skin when rubbed into feet.

Medicinal
☐ Violets have a calming and relaxing effect on the nervous system, act as a gentle laxative and help relieve coughs and colds.
☐ The flowers or leaves can be chewed to relieve a headache. Chew 5 at first then 3 more an hour later.
☐ A tea made from a quarter cup of violet leaves and flowers added to a cup of boiling water (stand for 5 minutes and strain) is effective in expelling mucus from the nose, throat, chest and lungs. A violet tea will also alleviate whooping cough and postnasal drip.
☐ Bruised violet leaves make a soothing poultice for skin infections and inflammations. A strong tea can be used as a wash for eczema and rashes.
☐ Africans use violet leaves as a cancer remedy. They chew the leaves and also use crushed leaves as a poultice for skin cancer and growths, binding them over the affected part. This remedy has also been used in Europe since the 12th century.

Culinary
☐ A syrup of violets can be added to puddings, creams, custards and ice-creams to add flavour and for its medicinal benefits. Boil up a cup of violet flowers in 2 cups of water. To this add 2 cups of sugar, and boil for 15 to 20 minutes until it thickens.
☐ Violets are best used on their own in cooking because they have such a subtle taste, but they combine well with lemon balm, bergamot, allspice, cinnamon, cloves, nutmeg and mint.
☐ Add violet flowers to salads for a lovely splash of colour; also use to garnish vegetable dishes.
☐ The petals may be crystallised to make a delicious and attractive decoration for cakes.
☐ Add violet leaves to salads and make into a tea. Pour 1 cup boiling water over a quarter cup of fresh leaves. Stand for 5 minutes, strain and sweeten with honey if liked.
☐ Make violet vinegar by half filling a jar with fresh violets, covering with good white vinegar, add a stick of cinnamon and stand in sun for ten days. Strain twice during that time and add fresh flowers and leaves. Finally bottle in screwtop jar. Add a few flowers to aid identification. Use for salad dressings or in the bath, and as a hair rinse.

WATERCRESS/BRONKORS
Nasturtium officinale
Family: Cruciferae

Land cress

Watercress is a wonderfully versatile herb that is also commercially important as a salad vegetable. It has a delicious peppery taste and is extremely high in vitamin C and other vitamins and minerals. As its name suggests, it likes moist conditions. (A variety known as land cress, Lepidium sativum, has the same properties as ordinary watercress and can be grown year-round in a cotton wool-lined tray or out in full sun in the garden.) It can be planted in cool, damp spots in the garden. Watercress is not indigenous to South Africa but has become half wild here and can often be found in streams, furrows and dams.

CULTIVATION
Watercress can be an annual or sometimes a biennial in favourable conditions.

Conditions: Likes partial shade and damp, swampy conditions. It does well in soils with a high lime content.

Propagation: Watercress can easily be grown from seed as long as the soil is not allowed to dry out. Propagation can also be done by rooted stems. It seeds itself readily along furrows and in swampy ground in spring. The ideal situation is along the edges of furrows in running water, but as this is seldom possible it may succeed under a dripping tap or grown in a pot in a bowl of water. If they are grown in stagnant water the plants will soon die. Spring and early summer are the best times for watercress – with another crop sown in March for winter picking.

Sprinkle seeds onto a moist patch of ground. Cover with a little sand and a fine sprinkling of compost. Shade with hessian and keep moist. Once the seeds are at the four-leaf stage remove the hessian, but keep the seedlings moist.

Containers: Land cress can be grown indoors on trays lined with wet cotton wool. Cut the sprouts off with scissors. Children particularly love growing it this way.

Size: Grows to a height of 15 cm.

Harvesting: Pick the outer lower leaves, or the side-shoot rosettes of leaves for salads.

Dos and don'ts: Watercress needs cool conditions, so if you live in a hot part of the country it is advisable to sow in autumn for a winter salad crop. It runs to seed easily, so keep picking in those first days of spring.

USES
Domestic
☐ Watercress that has gone to seed can be pulled up and used in compost making. It is one of the most remarkable compost breakers I know of – one bucketful will immediately break down a large heap.

☐ The Xhosa use watercress as an anthrax remedy for cattle.

Cosmetic
☐ Apply juice of watercress to a blemish or pimple for quick healing. Pulp leaves and stems and apply juice to the spot. Leave for 15 minutes and wash off with tepid water.

☐ Eat watercress or land cress frequently in the daily salad to keep the skin clear – it is an excellent blood cleanser.

Medicinal
☐ Because it is so high in vitamin C watercress is used as a treatment for scurvy. It is also effective in combating anaemia, rickets and weak eyesight. It is particularly good for the elderly as it is a stimulating herb and moves the circulation.

☐ Combined with honey, watercress makes a good cough remedy.

Culinary
☐ The most common culinary use of watercress is in salads or sandwiches, but it is superb in stir-fries and finely chopped in marinades for fish and lamb.

☐ Watercress can be used to make a tasty soup.

☐ Watercress makes a delicious vegetarian dish when steamed with spinach and served with a cheese sauce.

☐ Land cress is a superb salad ingredient.

WINTER SAVORY/MEERJARIGE BONEKRUID
Satureja montana
Family: Labiatae

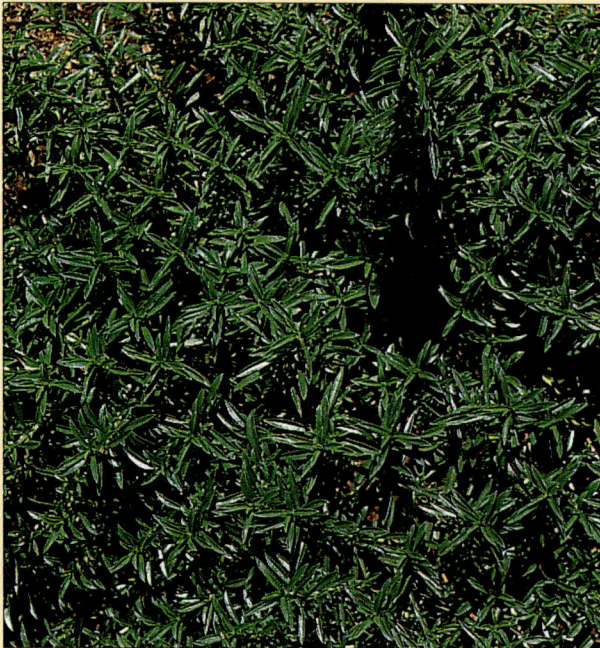

Winter savory has a lower, more spreading growth than summer savory and makes an ideal path edging in the herb garden. As its name suggests, this plant weathers winter well. It was used as a strewing plant in ancient times and has been used as a culinary herb for a very long time. The Romans added it to their sauces and vinegars, and believed it to have aphrodisiac qualities.

CULTIVATION
Winter savory is a hardy perennial plant that forms an excellent ground cover.

Conditions: Winter savory likes a light, well-drained soil and full sun.

Propagation: Cuttings or seeds. Cuttings may be taken at any time of year except the coldest months. It germinates fairly successfully from fresh seeds, but germination is slow. Plant out seedlings 30 cm apart and water well in first few weeks; thereafter once a week. Dig in a little compost round the roots from time to time. In summer it is a mass of tiny white flowers.

Size: Reaches a height of 15 to 20 cm.

Harvesting: Pick the leaves at any time of the year – the plant benefits from constant picking.

Dos and don'ts: Winter savory makes a useful edging plant. Plant it under roses to deter aphids, scale and mildew. It has a shallow rooting system so is excellent as an underplanting. You'll never need to spray your roses.

USES
Domestic
☐ The branches and leaves may be thrown on fires to provide an aromatic disinfectant. The tiny white flowers are an excellent addition to insect repelling potpourris.

Cosmetic
☐ The flowering top may be used in facial steams or baths to reduce greasiness in oily skin. Alternatively, make an astringent and skin cleanser by boiling 1 cup of leaves in 2 *l* of water for 15 minutes. Cool and strain, then use on pads of cotton wool.

Medicinal
☐ Make a tea from the leaves of winter savory to relieve coughs and colds. The standard brew is 1 cup of boiling water poured over a quarter cup of fresh leaves. Stand for 5 minutes then strain. Add lemon and honey.

☐ An alternative cold and flu recipe with winter savory may be made as follows: Add 10 ml dried winter savory to a litre of boiling water, then add one cinnamon stick and five cloves. Boil for exactly three minutes, then strain. Drink a glass morning, noon and night. 20 ml of fresh winter savory may be used instead of the dried variety.

☐ Like summer savory, this variety is beneficial for constipation and flatulence and helps regulate the bowels.

☐ Apply crushed leaves to wasp stings and insect bites.

Culinary
☐ The leaves of winter savory are a delicious addition to bean dishes.

☐ Savory is used commercially to flavour salami.

☐ Add to salt-free diets as its pungent flavour is a good salt substitute.

☐ Sprinkle on top of soups and sauces.

☐ Use savory to flavour vinegar.

WORMWOOD/ WILDE ALS

Artemisia absinthium, A. afra
Family: Compositae

African wormwood (A. afra)

Wormwood, one of the best-known medicinal herbs, belongs to the genus Artemisia, which also includes mugwort and southernwood. Like other members of the genus, it has a pungent smell. Wormwood also has a bitter taste, because of the presence of absinthe, which is used to make the famous green liqueur. It gets its name from its ability to get rid of worms. It has been known as an outstanding healing herb from very early times, when it was chosen as the symbol of health; in fact healers had the leaf painted on their doors as a sign of their profession. John the Baptist wore a woven girdle of wormwood, hence its other name, "St John's girdle." Artemisia afra, commonly known as wild wormwood or wilde als, grows wild in South Africa, and is a very widely used medicinal herb.

CULTIVATION

Artemisia afra (wilde als) is an attractive feathery grey-green shrub that is an asset to any garden.

Conditions: *A. afra* is very drought resistant and hardy, and will grow in any soil. It just needs occasional watering and cutting back.

Propagation: Wilde als can be propagated very quickly and easily. Take 10 cm cuttings, trim off excess leaves at the base of the stem, press into a prepared tray and keep moist until established. Transplant into larger pots and plant out when strong and bushy. Plant a metre apart as the bushes grow large, water once or twice weekly until they are growing well, thereafter once weekly.

Containers: *Artemisia afra* can be used as a pot plant if placed in a large tub, but must be trimmed frequently.

Size: *A. afra* grows to between 1 and 2 m.

Harvesting: Clip back plants to neaten them at the end of summer, and save the leaves.

Dos and don'ts: Do grow wilde als for a fast temporary hedge. Do grow it near hen houses for protection against lice, near cabbages to deter cabbage butterfly and near fruit trees to keep away fruit tree moth.

USES

Domestic

☐ Wilde als can be rubbed on the skin to act as an insect repellent, but test first in the case of tender skins. It can be placed in a bowl nearby for the same purpose, or rubbed onto window sills, etc. Crush frequently.

☐ It can be dried and powdered and sprinkled around ants' nests and fruit trees to deter ants and fruit flies. In its dried form it can help keep weevils out of stored grain. A liquid can be made to spray against aphids and mites. Take half a bucket of wilde als branches, well pressed down, and then fill the bucket with boiling water. Add a cupful of washing powder and allow to draw overnight. Strain and use as a spray.

☐ A bath of wilde als will chase fleas off a dog.

☐ Wilde als can be used in sachets and insect-repelling potpourris.

Cosmetic

☐ Some African tribes make a wash of the plant to treat skin complaints, and apply warmed leaves to draw pimples and boils. They also believe that if a brew is drunk it will cleanse the skin.

Medicinal

☐ Wilde als has been used medicinally for hundreds of years by the indigenous southern African peoples, and was also widely used by the early white settlers, probably because it closely resembles the European variety.

☐ Wilde als has an antiseptic, vermifuge (anti-worm) and narcotic effect and is used to relieve pain and for treating fevers, worms, constipation, coughs, sore throats, flu and jaundice. It also restores appetite, aids digestion, cures diarrhoea and dysentery.

☐ It is also known for its effectiveness in treating "women's complaints" such as morning sickness.

☐ Wilde als is wonderfully soothing if drunk for ear-ache and ear infections. The brew can be made by adding three 15-cm-long sprigs to 600 ml boiling water. Sweeten with honey to disguise its bitterness and take 10 ml morning and night for four days at the most. Wilde als is very potent, so it is important not to exceed the dosage. If too large or prolonged a dose is taken, it will dilate the blood vessels and have an effect on the heart.

☐ If you have toothache, pack the tooth with a leaf to ease the pain until you can get to a dentist.

YARROW/DUISENDBLAD
Achillea millefolium
Family: Compositae

Yarrow is indigenous to Europe and has been used for thousands of years to heal wounds. Achilles used the leaves and flowers to treat his soldiers after the Battle of Troy, hence its scientific name. Yarrow's healing power is reflected in the common names, among which are "soldier's wound wort," "knight milfoil," "nose bleed" and "carpenter's herb." Yarrow was used by the Druids to predict the weather, and by the Chinese to foretell the future.

There are several varieties of yarrow. The coarser leaved yellow Achillea filipendulina and Greek yarrow, Achillea ageratifolia, look good in flower arrangements but do not have the medicinal properties of common yarrow and should not be confused with it.

CULTIVATION

Yarrow is a hardy herbaceous perennial that is very attractive throughout the year, with masses of pink and white flowers in spring and summer.

Conditions: Yarrow is not fussy about its soil requirements but prefers a moderately rich and moist soil. It likes a sunny position.

Propagation: Dig side runners out and plant them in a new position. Separate and divide the clumps every third or fourth year and dig in some compost and old manure. Plant out 30 cm apart and water well.

Containers: Yarrow is not suitable for growing indoors, but makes a superb pot plant – plant in deep, wide pots and place in full sun.

Size: 30-60 cm.

Harvesting: Gather leaves any time of year and flowers in late summer (pick when they open for arrangements).

Dos and don'ts: Do plant yarrow near ailing plants to revive them as it helps them to resist disease and deepens their fragrance and flavour. An attractive border plant that grows well near vegetables, yarrow will attract butterflies to your garden.

USES

Domestic
☐ The leaves and flowers dry well and can be added to potpourri.
☐ Yarrow promotes decomposition and is a superb compost maker.

Cosmetic
☐ The fresh flowers can be made into an infusion for a facial steam, cleanser or tonic lotion. This infusion can also be used in the bath or as the basis of a face pack.

Medicinal
☐ Yarrow has long been known for its efficiency in healing wounds. Nowadays it is also used in the treatment of hypertension and coronary thrombosis.
☐ Yarrow's astringent properties make it ideal in cases of excessive menstruation and dysentery. It is also a diuretic. To make the standard brew (tea) pour a cup of boiling water over a quarter cup of fresh leaves and stand for 5 minutes. Strain and drink.
☐ A yarrow lotion can soothe haemorrhoids.
☐ The fresh leaves can be used pulped on eczema, skin rashes and scratches.
☐ The leaves can be warmed and placed behind the ear to relieve earache, or a salve can be made by melting cold cream and working in finely chopped yarrow flowers and a few leaves. A little beeswax can be added if necessary to help it solidify. Place a wad of this salve behind the ear and a rolled up, moistened leaf inside the ear, as well as a few drops of yarrow brew.
☐ Chewing the leaves helps relieve toothache – but make sure the juice is not swallowed.
☐ Yarrow is excellent for bringing down fever as it dilates the pores and promotes sweating. Fever sufferers can be given a yarrow bath as well as yarrow tea.

Culinary
☐ Yarrow is more renowned as a medicinal herb than a culinary one, but its leaf has a spicy spinach-like taste and is rich in vitamins and minerals. It can be used alone as a vegetable or in stuffings (especially for poultry) and cream sauces. It goes well with curries and is superb used sparingly in salads, particularly beetroot salad – on its own or with other herbs.

INDEX